Mr. Secretary of State

STUDIES IN
POLITICAL
SCIENCE

Preface

The shift from isolation to leadership in American policy has transformed the secretary of state from a national to a world figure. Abroad, as well as at home, the resignation of Secretary Dulles and the appointment of Christian Herter were watched with a sense of deep involvement. No appointment by President Kennedy after the election of 1960 aroused as much speculation and interest, both in this country and among our friends and enemies in other lands, as that of Dean Rusk to the Department of State. Upon the secretary of state more than any other free-world statesman, except the president, rest the eyes of all mankind.

The office of secretary of state has been shaped as much by the men who have filled it and their presidents as by the exigencies of foreign and domestic affairs. With a wide assortment of human qualities, they have reacted to the environment in which they have found themselves, whether it was a demanding public, a hostile Congress, China under the heel of Japan in 1937, or the world under the menace of international communism since 1945. As a consequence, the office has been changing and growing. In detailing the personal side of the office, I have pointed out significant developments and problems of its past and present. Recently there has been talk of a reorganization of the processes of advising the president in matters of foreign policy which would affect the secretary's position in important ways. In the last chapter, I have summarized developments of the past and focused attention on new proposals for change.

I have taken most of the information contained in this volume from the biographies, autobiographies, and memoirs of the secretaries of state. Periodical and newspaper publications have also proved useful. The personal observations of men close to the office have been sought and in some instances obtained; for this assistance I am grateful. I acknowledge further the advantages provided in the writing of this account by a fellowship grant from the Woods Foundation at the University of Nebraska.

Norman L. Hill

NOVEMBER, 1962

Contents

· I ·

At the President's Right

When urging Thomas Jefferson to take the post, President Washington wrote with his usual restraint, "I consider the office of Secretary for the Department of State as very important on many accounts." Since its beginning, it has rated as the top position in the president's cabinet, and its incumbent has occupied the seat of honor at the president's right. From 1789, when the Constitution went into effect, until the present—from John Jay (a holdover Secretary from the Articles of Confederation, not commissioned under the Constitution) to Dean Rusk—fifty-three men have held "this perilous office," as Edmund Randolph called it.

Most secretaries have discovered that the position at the president's right is by no means a sinecure. After being commissioned Secretary of State on September 21, 1817, John Quincy Adams wrote a poem of six stanzas, one of which was as follows:

Extend, all-seeing God, thy hand,
In mercy still decree,
And make to bless my native land
An instrument of me.

He soon found himself a very busy instrument; his job was "onerous in the extreme." After six months of work he wrote to his mother, "Business crowds upon me from day to day requiring instantaneous attention, and in such variety that unless everything is disposed of just as it occurs, it escapes the memory and runs into the account of arrears."

John Hay was well aware, as any man should be, before he took over the office of the weight of the load he was about to shoulder. Writing to Samuel Mather, he said, "I have never been so oppressed by a sense of inadequacy before. I feel as if I had been drawn into a match with Corbett and the day of the match was drawing on, and all my hope was to be knocked out by an early blow which would not kill me." He was on the verge of being knocked out several times during his six and one-half years at the Department, and finally he died while yet in office. No one can know how much his onerous duties hastened his death at the age of sixty-seven. We do know, however, that he spent many days, even years, at the job when he did not feel up to it.

Wartime secretaries have always been deluged by new duties. To some extent Secretary Seward's busy hours were the result of the many tasks he undertook relating to the Civil War, tasks which did not come properly within the scope of his Department. No doubt it was true, too, that he liked to tell people how busy he was. Unquestionably, Secretary Hull's burdens increased enormously during World War II, as he and the Department tackled problems of inter-Allied cooperation and of the peace to come, although his nearly twelve years of service were a continuous succession of emergencies. He remained at his desk evenings and Sundays much of the time. As he said, "Mine was an aggravated case of the ox in the ditch on the Sabbath." Sunday noons when he returned to his hotel rooms he "listened to Mrs. Hull's gentle remonstrance, 'Sunday is a day of rest.' "

The vast majority of secretaries would agree with Edward Everett, one of President Fillmore's Department of

State heads, when he wrote to his wife, "I thought I knew what work was—but this is the beatem." Writing in the *Reader's Digest* (July, 1947), John Hersey described without too much exaggeration the kind of man ideally equipped for the post as one with "a mind combining the powers of Albert Einstein, Benjamin Franklin and the I-B-M-Automatic Sequence-Controlled Calculator; and a body blending the merits of Glen Davis and Methuselah." Needless to say, the fifty-three secretaries, being human, have all fallen short of this ideal.

The duties of the secretary of state have grown both in numbers and in complexity since 1789. His present official activities, discussed with some detail in later chapters, include the following:

1. advising the president on major questions of policy (consulting with him and keeping him informed);
2. making decisions on policy questions not important enough to take to the president or on issues about which the president has given him authority;
3. serving as the administrative head of the State Department;
4. attending meetings of the cabinet, the National Security Council, and interdepartmental boards;
5. making appropriate contacts with the Congress and with the public in order to explain and justify and to elicit support for what the administration is doing or is proposing to do;
6. negotiating treaties and agreements with nations on outstanding problems;
7. consulting with top officials in the Department, diplomats from other countries, members of Congress, and others;
8. traveling abroad on good-will trips or on negotiating missions.

Besides the actual business of his office, the secretary faces many social demands that consume time and energy. Many of these are so closely tied up with his official activities that they cannot be separated. He is especially obligated to the foreign diplomatic corps in Washington, whose members are in a special way the guests of the nation. Foreign dignitaries—kings, presidents, prime ministers, and foreign ministers—visiting in this country require the attention of the secretary. In addition, there are many social functions in the capital to which the secretary and his wife are invited as a matter of course. However, there is an element of choice in the less official invitations which he gives and receives, and it is probable that, as Mr. Acheson has said, more social events "are avoidable than are avoided." Secretary Hull was one of many secretaries who tried to reduce such engagements to a minimum. He explained to the foreign diplomatic corps in Washington that were he to "go out almost daily to luncheons and dinners with you," he would then "be unable to see you and confer with you except to a limited extent and you'll have to see my Assistant Secretary instead." His decision to see them less often socially and to make himself more available officially did not reduce his social obligations as much as he had hoped, especially after World War II started and brought to Washington a steady parade of high officials from abroad for whom luncheons and dinners became the duty of the host nation. Although they are time consuming, the social contacts of the secretary with foreign diplomats and dignitaries and with high officials in our own government, if not carried to an excess, are helpful in paving the way for the serious business discussions that will come later.

Upon coming into office, Secretary Dulles was critical of his predecessor, Secretary Acheson, for not freeing himself enough from administrative problems to have more time to think, and he stated his intention to change things. No evidence is at hand to show that Dulles succeeded in changing the upper echelons of the Department in such a way as to free himself; to the contrary, he was constantly on the go. On the basis of his own experience, Mr. Acheson expressed skepticism about Mr. Dulles's project to get relief from the burden of work by "reorganization in the very highest echelons." Poking fun at the idea, he said that it all reminded him of "the signs which, for a time, hung on the walls of some offices urging 'THINK'—and of the addendum written in pencil on one of them, 'OR THWIM.' " In his opinion, about all a secretary can do to lighten his burden is to use the time he has more wisely. The problem, he feels, is one of a "disciplined and intelligent choice of how time is used."

In its salary as well as in its heavy responsibilities, the office of secretary of state would be a disappointment to sinecure seekers. Indeed the whole department has traditionally operated on an inadequate budget. Senator Dana walked over to the office of Secretary John Quincy Adams to find out why in 1820 the Department cost twice as much as it had in 1800. The Secretary explained that the salaries of his clerks were on a mere subsistence level and quite inadequate for the skill required. Although foreign correspondence had increased only moderately, correspondence with the states of the Union had expanded a great deal. In 1800 it could be contained in two or three octavos and one folio, whereas in 1820 twenty volumes were required. In 1820 the 230 members of Congress made five times as many requests for information and for documents as were submitted in 1800 by the 130 members. Mr. Adams explained that the Department badly needed one or two more clerks at that very time. The Department has usually been given more money than Congress considered justifiable, but less than was needed.

The secretary's salary, like the Department's budgetary allowance, has lagged behind actual needs. When Senator Dana demanded an explanation of the Department's budget, Secretary Adams explained that his own salary of $6,000 was from $4,000 to $5,000 short of the amount he had to spend for personal and official purposes. If Congress wished him to increase the amount he was paying to serve the country, he would do so, however reluctantly. During his seven and one-half years in office, Secretary Adams dipped heavily into his own private funds, estimated at $100,000 when he took office.

The first secretary of state was paid $3,500 a year. The salary was gradually increased, first to $5,000 in 1799; by 1853 it reached $8,000, where it remained for more than fifty years. Many secretaries took the position at a financial loss, often so great that no government could hope either to prevent it or to repay it. Elihu Root, for example, went from legal fees of $200,000 a year to $8,000 as State Department head in 1905. Just before Philander Knox became Secretary under President Taft in 1909, the Congress raised the salary to $12,000, but Knox was unable to accept the increase because he had been a member of the Senate when the change was voted. Under the Constitution a member of Congress may not be appointed to any civil office whose emoluments were increased while he was in the Senate or House of Representatives. None of the able constitutional lawyers in the government had thought of the problem until it arose. The only solution was to repeal the relevant section of the law and drop the secretary's salary to $8,000. In 1911, when the six-year term for which he had been elected to the Senate expired, the Congress restored the $12,000 salary provision.

Secretary Acheson's salary was $22,500, but of this amount he had to give back $7,500 in the form of income taxes. He found the remaining $15,000 inadequate to his needs, even though it was supplemented by government assistance for the official entertainment of foreign visitors. Recent secretaries have been drawing $25,000 a year, less income tax withholdings.

Dean Rusk came into the office at a considerable financial sacrifice. Although the Rockefeller Foundation has never made public the salary of its president, well-founded rumor placed it between $50,000 and $75,000 a year. The Secretary's financial problems are not lessened by inherited wealth, as they were for some of his predecessors. He was not born into affluence, and his career spent mainly as a teacher and government official never gave him a chance to amass a fortune of his own.

·II·

Appointment

In the selection of his secretary of state, a president will take several considerations into account. Like a man choosing a wife, he may be influenced by material advantage, his own and his party's future prosperity. He may be the victim of a shot-gun marriage where he has no free choice and is forced by the circumstances of politics to team up with a given politician whether he wants to or not. Because of the close personal relationships that exist between him and his secretary, a president may emphasize in his appointee a mate with whom he can work harmoniously, without the tensions that may lead to a divorce. He will be concerned, more than ever recently, that his nominee be proficient in the art of diplomacy, capable of serving him well as cook and housekeeper.

Although political gain has been discernible in most appointments, it has not followed that politician-secretaries have all been failures. President Jackson said about his appointment of Martin Van Buren, "I called him to the Department of State influenced by the general wish and expectation of the (Democratic) Republican Party throughout the Union." The choice was nevertheless a good one. Charles Evans Hughes, selected by President Harding in part because he was acceptable to factions within the Republican Party caused by the League of Nations issue, turned out to be an exceptionally able secretary.

James G. Blaine's first appointment was based on considerations, political and personal, often conspicuous both before and since his time. In the Republican National Convention of 1880, Grant and Blaine were the two leading candidates for the party nomination for the presidency, but a deadlock in the voting brought Garfield's name to the front as a way out by compromise. Blaine threw his support to Garfield, with the result that Garfield was nominated. Added to the political debt thus incurred by President Garfield were the excellent personal relationship and friendship between the two men. They had entered Congress at the same time and, during their parallel careers over many years, had come to have confidence in each other. In the light of these circumstances, it was obvious that Blaine would be offered a chance at the Department of State. Indeed, the President gave his old friend a choice of posts within his administration, and Blaine picked the Department of State. In accepting the position the new Secretary wrote to his chief, "I could not enter your Cabinet if I did not believe in you as a man and love you as a friend."

Years earlier, in 1824, Henry Clay had become Secretary of State for President John Quincy Adams, partly at least in payment of a political debt contracted in a somewhat different way. Clay had been a president-maker no less than had Blaine. In the presidential election no candidate received a majority vote in the Electoral College, with the result that the election went over to the House of Representatives, as the Constitution requires. In the House, Henry Clay, one of the candidates, withdrew his name and backed John Quincy Adams, thereby making Adams the new President. This infuriated General Jackson and his cohorts, for the General had had a plurality of the popular vote, even though he failed to get a majority in the Electoral College. When President Adams appointed Henry Clay his Secretary of State, Jackson's friends suspected a secret deal, which appeared even more ignominious because in those days a secretary of state was regarded as strategically placed to become the next president. Cries of "bargain and corruption" and "bargain and sale" were heard throughout the country.

The idea of discharging a political debt was doubtless in President Wilson's mind when he appointed William Jennings Bryan, in addition to the incontrovertible fact that Bryan had for sixteen years been the leader of the Democratic Party and therefore could not be overlooked if party harmony were to be preserved. As Mr. Dooley remarked, Wilson would fare better to have Bryan "in his bosom than on his back." The relations between the two men had not always been friendly. In 1907 Woodrow Wilson, writing to Mr. Joline, made a widely publicized statement to the effect that he would like to "knock Mr. Bryan once for all into a cocked hat." Bryan was, as Wilson saw it at that time, a demagogue. In 1911 this breach between the two Democrats was at least partially healed, as Wilson had come to see that Bryan's heart was on the side of the people. Early in 1911 the two men and their wives dined together, and soon thereafter Wilson in public spoke well of his fellow Democrat as a leader who had "borne the heat and burden of the day." In 1912, at a Jackson Day dinner, Wilson proposed that the two men apologize to each other for having "ever suspected or antagonized each other."

It was at the Baltimore Convention of the Democratic Party in 1912 that Woodrow Wilson became indebted to Bryan. During the early part of the Convention, Bryan supported Champ Clark, continuing to do so until the cause was clearly lost; then he gave his strength to Wilson with decisive effect. Tumulty relates that during the Convention, when Bryan's powerful position was quite apparent, politician McCombs called Wilson on the phone and said that he could get the nomination for him if he would agree not to place the Nebraska orator in his cabinet. According to Tumulty, "Wilson came back into the room from the telephone very pale and said, 'I have just refused the nomination' and then told me what McCombs proposed. I asked him what he said to McCombs and Wilson replied, 'I told him to go to h—!' " Nominee Wilson's debt was augmented considerably by the fact that Bryan gave a large number of speeches during the campaign. As another president-maker, Bryan was invited to become Secretary of State. He accepted with alacrity.

A political appointment of another type is illustrated by President Lincoln's selection of William Seward as his Secretary. The President had no political debt to pay, but he was well aware that his appointee was the outstanding man in the Republican Party, more so than he himself at that time. A few months before the National Party Convention met, Seward was expected to be made the Party's candidate, but it did not work out. On December 8, 1860, the President-elect wrote to the New York politician, "I now offer you the place in the hope that you will accept it, and with the belief that your position in the public eye, your integrity, ability, learning and great experience, all combine to render it an appointment pre-eminently fit to be made." The offer did not come as a surprise to Seward and was not received with enthusiasm, but it was accepted, apparently with the thought in mind that he could steer the Lincoln administration through the stormy times ahead.

One of the bafflements of the political observer is that he can read men's motives only indirectly by their doings. This limitation places him in the dangerous position that he may draw unwarranted conclusions. For this reason, and in the interest of fairness, let us say that these appointments made by Presidents John Quincy Adams, James Garfield, Woodrow Wilson, and Abraham Lincoln to the office of secretary of state appear in part at least to have been politically motivated. Because there is no way of knowing the thoughts of presidents, evidence in support of such a statement must be largely circumstantial. That the political motive was often accompanied by others is probable. President Adams may well have regarded Henry Clay's qualifications for the post outstanding, as in truth they were, for Clay had one of the finest intellects in politics. Certainly President Garfield had the highest esteem for James G. Blaine, both as a person and as a statesman, and would consider the appointment to be good for the nation. President Wilson undoubtedly saw in Bryan's appointment a means to party unity, a political imperative if his program of reforms were to be adopted by the Congress.

Personal motives appear to have been dominant in some presidential selections of secretaries of state. Presidents want men with whom they can work, whose thinking will be in accord with their own, or perhaps supplement their own. Reference has been made to the friendly intimacy between President Garfield and James G. Blaine. When President Theodore Roosevelt named Elihu Root to the State Department he wrote to Senator Beveridge, "I wished Root as Secretary of State partly because I am extremely fond of him and prize his companionship as his advice, but primarily because I think that in all the country he is the best man for the position."

In a letter asking Secretary Lansing to step down from the office, President Wilson wrote in 1920 that he wanted for the post somebody "whose mind would more willingly go along with mine." The President had had enough contact with men whose minds had moved in the opposite direction when Bryan and Lansing had worked under his direction, and, ill as he was, he naturally sought an end to conflict. Bainbridge Colby was the President's choice. Colby had been a member of the Progressive Party in 1912, but in 1916 he became a Democrat and brought strong support to candidate Wilson. The motive of paying a political debt may have played a part in the decision to make Colby his Secretary, but certainly not a large part, for the President was engrossed in his present problem. Besides, he had already given Colby wartime positions on the United Shipping Board and the Emergency Fleet Corporation. A year or so before Lansing's resignation, Wilson had told Colby by letter, "I know of no public servant whose attitude and ability I more admire than your own."

The competence of a prospective appointee has no doubt been a consideration in the mind of every president, although in the old days, when foreign affairs were less critical than now, the chief executive appeared less influenced by ability or expertness than by politics and personal compatibility. This was especially true when a president expected to keep a tight hold on foreign policy himself, and a first-class secretary might be more obstructive than helpful.

Although President Washington expected to be active in foreign policy, he selected his first secretary on the basis of competence. Three men in 1789 seemed to possess the necessary background in diplomacy and the ability for the position of secretary of state: John Jay, who was actually serving in the office as a hold over from the Articles of Confederation; John Adams; and Thomas Jefferson. Jay preferred the position of chief justice of the Supreme Court and Adams was already the nation's vice-president. This left Jefferson as the logical man for the post. President Washington offered it to him while he was in France serving as Minister. Showing no enthusiasm, Jefferson accepted and was commissioned on September 26, but he did not take office until March 22, 1790. Although the President's two later appointments to the position were not politically inspired, they did not draw upon diplomatic experience either. Edmund Randolph was an eminent Virginian whose official contact with foreign affairs had been limited to his legal opinions on problems of international law given as the nation's first Attorney General. Timothy Pickering's nomination was a desperation measure after the President had offered the post to four other men only to receive rejections; Pickering had had no experience in diplomacy and accepted the offer at first on an interim basis while continuing to serve as Secretary of War.

An effort to find experience and ability appeared to be uppermost in President Benjamin Harrison's appointment of John Foster, after Blaine's resignation, and in McKinley's selection of John Hay. Although both of them stood well in the Republican Party, neither had significant political influence. Both men, on the other hand, were well trained by experience in diplomacy. The selection of Robert Lansing for Secretary by President Wilson in 1915, after Bryan's resignation, seemed superficially to belong in a similar category; in any case, it was nonpolitical. The difference was that Lansing, unlike Foster and Hay, had had but little diplomatic experience, and his background was related to the legal aspects of international relations. He had been counsel for the United States in several arbitration cases, and, immediately before his nomination, he had been Counselor in the Department of State. President Wilson was not interested in Lansing as a politician, nor even as a diplomat, for the President intended to manage foreign affairs himself; he sought in his appointee a person who could advise on the legal problems arising in our neutrality policy during World War I and manage the Department in its manifold activities. When Lansing hesitated in accepting the appointment, the President told him in a letter, "By experience and training you are especially equipped to conduct the foreign affairs of the United States. This under present conditions is far more important than political influence." In justifying the selection, Secretary McAdoo of the Treasury Department said, "He was the best material at hand, he could put diplomatic notes into proper form and advise on international law, and the President had determined for the future to be his own secretary of state." "A high-class clerk," according to another commentator, was what the President sought.

Since World War II, as the environment of world politics has grown more complicated, a new trend in presidential selections of State Department heads has been apparent. Preoccupation with the Russo-Chinese challenge to our security, anxiety for the future of the newly emergent nations, concern over United Nations affairs, and the obligation to keep up with the quickened pace of events everywhere have combined to require the president to think less about politics or personal whim and more about diplomatic experience and expertness. Never before in our history has there been such a procession of nonpolitical appointees. Six of the last seven secretaries—Edward Stettinius, Jr., General Marshall, Dean Acheson, John Foster Dulles, Christian Herter, and Dean Rusk—have been men of substantial backgrounds in world affairs and had little or nothing to add to the president's political strength except a fair chance of doing an efficient job. The other, James Byrnes, had spent most of his life as a politician, and the surmise seems fair that among the considerations in President Truman's mind were Byrnes' strength in the Senate (which would help to ensure approval of the United Nations Charter, soon to come up), his prestige in the party and in the nation, his diplomatic experience at Yalta, and his qualifications as a person next in line for the presidency. Christian Herter, too, had been a politician, but not a prominent one, and apparently his appointment was not dictated by politics. His experience as Under Secretary would have made him a logical man for consideration by any president in the midst of a crisis as serious as that over Berlin, raised a few months earlier by Soviet Russia.

In Dean Rusk, President Kennedy found, so he said, a man who would "bring to this high office the long view of a student of world affairs, the concern for peace shared by all who have known war at first hand, and a practical working experience in the conduct of our foreign relations." Mr. Rusk had held several different posts in the Department of State between 1946 and 1951, most important of which were Assistant Secretary of State for Far Eastern Affairs and Deputy Undersecretary in charge of operations.

In selecting a secretary of state, a president may or may not seek the advice of others, depending on circumstances and the president's frame of mind at the time. The extent of such consultations cannot be fully known, for often they have not been publicized; nor is there complete information as to how frequently initiative in the way of suggestions comes from the outside, as in 1844, when Congressman Wise went to President Tyler to urge the selection of John Calhoun. The fact that retiring secretaries have been called upon to suggest successors has been brought out several times. Retiring Secretary Webster, shortly before his death in office on October 24, 1852, advised President Fillmore to name Edward Everett to fill out the few remaining months of his term. When Elihu Root left office only thirty-seven days before the termination of President Roosevelt's four-year term in 1909, he recommended Robert Bacon, his Assistant Secretary of State to succeed him; and, before William H. Taft assumed the presidency in the same year, Mr. Root suggested Philander Knox as the new State Department head.

After announcing the appointment of Dean Rusk at a news conference on December 12, 1960, President-elect Kennedy was asked how it had happened that the appointee's name had come to his attention and whether ex-Secretary Acheson had suggested him. The President-elect replied that Mr. Rusk had been recommended "by a good many people in varied parts of the country and of varied responsibility who spoke extremely highly of him." Asked how long he had known the man, Kennedy replied, "I have just come to know him. I met him for the first time this week."

Recipients of presidential proposals for nomination as secretary of state have rarely accepted with an eagerness equal to that of James G. Blaine. The wooings of chief executives have often met with a lukewarm "yes" or even a chilly "no." President Washington's first appointee, Thomas Jefferson, replied to a letter offering him the post that he would rather remain in Paris where he was serving as Minister but would be willing to sacrifice his own inclinations if the President thought that he would be more useful as Secretary of State. John Marshall debated with himself for nearly two weeks before accepting President Adams' overtures and then resigned after a brief tenure of less than nine months. Daniel Webster had no desire for any administrative position when President William H. Harrison sent him a surprise letter making the proposal, and he considered the matter for eleven days before writing a favorable reply. Shortly after William Evarts agreed to be Secretary for President Hayes, he wrote in a letter to Edward Pierrepont, "You see my running away from political employment has not ended any better than Jonah's escape from preaching at Nineveh, and I am now in the whale's belly, hoping some day to be cast on dry land."

No man has gone into the office with more reluctance and doubt than did John Hay. While visiting friends at Surrenden, Ambassador Hay received a cable from President McKinley saying that Secretary of State Day had resigned and asking him to take the position. Sixty years old at the time and not in the best of health, he feared the strain of the office and much preferred his London post. A sheet of note paper records Hay's cabled message of acceptance, and on the opposite page was a pencilled note of refusal never dispatched: "It would have been the dearest wish of my heart to be associated with you in that way, but my health will not permit it." Henry Adams said that Hay "shouldered his pack and started for home," and ". . . it was the gloomiest acquiescence he ever smiled."

Offers of appointment have been extended by presidents in different ways. According to Secretary Hull in his *Memoirs,* President Roosevelt stopped over in Washington to see him on the way from Warm Springs, Georgia, in January, 1933. Without any unnecessary words the President-elect offered him the secretaryship of state. Hull records, "I was really almost thunderstruck." He had not known that he was being considered for the position and had expected, as he said, that his career would continue on indefinitely in the Senate. Before making a final decision he wanted thirty days in which to think it over, a request which Roosevelt granted. Then in February he met with the President-elect again to clarify a few points. He wanted to know "how well we can and will work in complete cooperation." Then Hull explained in detail his conception of the office, making clear that he wanted to have a direct part in policy-making to the point of being free to recommend to the President but without impinging on Roosevelt's right to make final decisions on policy. The President-elect agreed with this conception of the office, and the two shook hands. They did not discuss the substance of policy at that time because "We had discussed foreign relations so much in the past, especially during the later twenties when I used to meet him as he came through Washington, that we thoroughly knew each other's views in the main." On February 21, Roosevelt announced his selection of a secretary of state, and Hull thereafter made public his desire to improve international trade by means of reciprocal agreements, a subject dear to his heart and the immediate objective of his effort.

Dean Acheson has described the offer to him of the secretaryship by President Truman at the end of November, 1948. He had been requested to stop in to see the President at Blair House and complied, thinking that he was to discuss the work of the first Hoover Commission, of which he was the Vice-Chairman. Acheson was surprised at the President's offer and "asked that we discuss the matter for a while." To a remark that it would be difficult to follow such a tower of strength as Secretary Marshall had been, "The President replied that without doubt there were people in the country more capable of being Secretary of State than I was, and more capable of being President than he was." After further discussion, Acheson "was sent off to sleep on the problem and to answer in the morning."

Never has a presidential nominee failed to receive Senate confirmation, as required by the Constitution, although one president at least, President Madison, desisted from sending to the Senate the name of the man he most wanted, Albert Gallatin, because he had reason to believe that the vote would be adverse. The presumption in the Senate is in favor of confirmation, and this is as it should be, for the president, responsible for his administration, should be free to select his own supporting officials. Usually confirmation is assured and fast, as speedy as that of Secretary Byrnes, whose name went to the Senate on a Saturday (June 30, 1945) and was approved the following Monday (July 2). Only occasionally has the Senate made an issue over a president's nominee.

The Senate was disposed to hold up President Wilson's

nomination of Bainbridge Colby, partly because the feud between the Chief Executive and the upper chamber of Congress was still raging. In addition, Colby's shift during his earlier career from the Republican Party to the Progressive Party and later to the Democratic Party had left him virtually a man without a party, unable to count on solid support from any quarter. The Senate took its time on the issue: the nomination came from the President on February 25; the Foreign Relations Committee did not report favorably until March 20, and the Senate did not approve until March 23. Fortunately, this style of politics has not often obstructed the nation's business.

· III ·

Tenure

The expectation is that secretaries will serve throughout the term of the presidents who appoint them, but in fact few have done so. Those who have left before the end of the president's term have usually quit voluntarily, but a considerable number were hurried off by death, illness, or the strong hands of presidents anxious for political or personal reasons to be rid of them. The fact that there have been thirty-four presidents from Washington to Kennedy and fifty-three secretaries from Jay to Rusk proves that the exits from the office have been put to use. In his eight years of office, President Washington had four secretaries; President Truman had the same number in slightly less than eight years. Single-term President Tyler had three, and President McKinley during his four years and six months had the same number, each more than any other president serving for an equal period of time.

The record of secretaries in the matter of tenure has not been uniformly creditable. The position is one in which the incumbent can and does learn by experience, so that the exit of a veteran secretary from office can be a distinct loss to the nation. Moreover, it creates uncertainty in American foreign policy both at home and abroad. Even if the president continues the same basic policy, as will be quite probable, the methods of the new appointee in negotiating and in working with the Congress and with the diplomats of other nations will be different and confusing. To be sure, most resignations of secretaries have been for good reasons. Some, however, have been for no better reason than to take a different position.

Among the common causes of the termination of a secretary's services has been the inauguration of a new president. Cause and effect in this matter are quite predictable if the new occupant of the White House brings into power a different political party from that which has hitherto governed. When John F. Kennedy and the Democratic Party replaced President Eisenhower and the Republican Party after the election of 1960, it was a foregone conclusion that Secretary Herter would be out. Even when a new president does not carry a new party into power, a secretary will offer his resignation in order to give the president a fair opportunity to have his own man working with him. A resignation under these circumstances may, of course, be rejected and the incumbent asked to stay on. When the president leaves office by way of death, the incoming president is similarly given a chance to select a new slate of departmental heads.

Although several secretaries have resigned because the president requested them to do so, only one has been discharged. The difference is primarily one of form or procedure, but it carries the implication that, if a sharp hint to a secretary or even an open request to resign is not enough, the chief executive may wield a final blow. Timothy Pickering was the only Secretary to receive such a blow, summarily dismissed as he was by President Adams. Pickering had gone from the War Department into the State Department with hesitation and largely to accommodate President Washington, who had appointed him. His background and interests were more in military matters than in diplomacy. When John Adams became President, he retained Pickering as his Secretary of State, although he knew that the Secretary was not keen on preventing the diplomatic rupture with France from degenerating into war.

As time passed, the relations between Pickering and President Adams grew worse and worse. The Secretary was gruff and undiplomatic in his methods, calling the French Government "devils out of pandemonium" and displaying contempt for the Spanish Minister. The ostensible reason for the Secretary's dismissal was that he favored war with France and tried to prevent the President from sending a second conciliatory mission to Paris. The President had lost confidence in his Secretary long before this, however, knowing among other things that Pickering had been consulting with Alexander Hamilton secretly about foreign affairs.

On May 10, 1800, President Adams wrote to the Secretary asking for his resignation. Pickering refused to resign. At this point Adams wielded the hatchet which every president has at hand for use when dissatisfied with the performance of an appointee: he discharged Pickering. In a note dated May 12, the Chief Executive notified Pickering that for "Divers causes and conditions essential to the administration of the Department of State, you are hereby discharged from any further service as Secretary of State." If any doubt had existed before as to the relationship which a secretary bears to his chief, it must have been dispelled by this act.

At least two secretaries since the time of Pickering have been requested to resign rather than discharged outright, a procedure which is a little more face-saving to the victim. In 1920, President Wilson asked for the resignation of Secretary Lansing because of serious differences, personal and political, that had arisen between them. Many years earlier, President Madison had requested the resignation of Secretary Smith, and no one could doubt the propriety of his action. Madison had appointed Smith with reluctance in the first place because a group of senators had supported him rather than Albert Gallatin, the President's preference. A second reason for Madison's request was the factional strife in the Cabinet. Gallatin, then his esteemed Secretary of the Treasury, was determined to leave unless Smith were eliminated. Still another motive, and not the least, was the inefficient service rendered by the Secretary of State; it was so inefficient that Henry Adams, writing of the period, could say, "The State Department stood helpless in the face of intolerable insults from all the European belligerents."

When a president and his secretary are at odds, a request for the latter's resignation is rarely needed; usually, the secretary will relieve the deadlock by taking the initiative himself and leaving. This, for instance, was Bryan's procedure in 1915 when he and President Wilson were in disagreement over American neutrality policy. If a secretary cannot conscientiously support presidential policy, the better part of wisdom is to resign and give his chief a chance to get someone who can.

Only one secretary of state has resigned under a cloud of suspicion. Edmund Randolph had spent his life in the legal profession and enjoyed the distinction of being President Washington's first Attorney General. From an eminent Virginian family, with an impressive record as Attorney General and Governor of Virginia, head of the delegation from Virginia to the Constitutional Convention in 1787, and the first Attorney General of the United States, he was a man with an enviable reputation when he took over the Department of State on January 2, 1794. During his tenure of a little more than a year and one-half he encountered some of the most serious diplomatic problems of our early history. Our declaration of neutrality in the war in Europe angered the French without placating the English. Problems with Revolutionary France, with Citizen Genet, and with Gouverneur Morris, our Minister in France, were vexing in the extreme. With England our relationships were equally critical, and the Jay Mission, itself a controversial question, was sent to reconcile the two nations. In dealing with these delicate issues, Secretary Randolph worked hard and was as effective as might reasonably have been expected.

In the midst of these burdens of his office, Randolph found himself caught up in a political scandal, for which he is usually more remembered than for his accomplishments, although his guilt was never established. Dispatches of Fauchet, the French Minister to the United States, reflecting upon the Secretary's integrity, were captured by the British and later found their way into the hands of President Washington. They seemed to show that the Secretary had secretly conspired with the French Minister to defeat the Jay Treaty, and they intimated, without specifically saying so, that Randolph had offered information in exchange for French gold.

President Washington's method of handling the matter was not to discuss it with his Secretary in private, as he might have done, but to take up the dispatch with the other Cabinet members and then at a later meeting of the entire Cabinet to confront Randolph with the document. The President took the dispatch from his pocket, handed it to his Secretary, and asked for an explanation. After a few verbal exchanges, which did not get out of hand, Washington asked him to leave the room while the other members of the Cabinet talked over the affair. This angered Randolph, who felt that he had not had a proper hearing. He left and on the same day tendered his resignation.

Another difficulty, less serious, was that, when Randolph left office, the State Department's funds were found to be deficient to the extent of $49,154.89. At that time the secretary was the disburser of funds for foreign relations and personally responsible for any losses sustained. No criminal charges were made, and there was no evidence of any personal irregularity; the fact that Randolph was poor and had to borrow $2,000 after leaving the Department was in itself a measure of exoneration. Suit was brought against Randolph to establish his liability, and an arbitrator found that he owed the government $53,162.89. Some payment was made, but part of the obligation passed on to his heirs and plagued them for many years.

Ill health and death have forced a number of secretaries from office. The first to die in office was Abel P. Upshur, who sustained a fatal accident on board the battleship *Princeton* on February 28, 1844. Daniel Webster,

Walter Gresham, John Hay, and John Foster Dulles also left office by the solemn route of death. Cordell Hull resigned in ill health, unable to continue his work.

Ostensibly, illness has at times been the reason for resignation when in fact it was minor to other considerations; this, of course, is a trick not peculiar to secretaries of state. Secretary Byrnes gave no reason other than health to justify his resignation, although President Truman later brought out in his *Memoirs* that he had reprimanded his Secretary several times for overlooking presidential authority in conducting foreign affairs. Byrnes's letter of resignation was dated April 16, 1946. In it he stressed the burden of his work, saying, "I have found it necessary to work long hours six and at times seven days a week." He continued, "Last week I had a medical examination. I was advised that I must 'slow down.' I know myself. I cannot slow down as long as I hold public office, particularly the office of Secretary of State." He fixed July 1 as the date on which he wished the resignation to become effective because he wanted first to finish up in Paris the work of making peace treaties with the German satellites of World War II. Inability to finish the work by that time led him to postpone the effective date to "January 10 or as soon thereafter as my successor is appointed or qualified."

In a letter written on January 7, 1947, to his Secretary, President Truman maintained the façade of ill-health as the reason for the resignation. He then accepted the resignation "with great reluctance and heartfelt regret" and complimented Byrnes for a job well done. Problems of the utmost moment, so the President wrote, had been handled "with rare tact and judgment and—when necessary—firmness and tenacity of purpose." Admiration was expressed for the "steadying hand" with which the Secretary had coped with the baffling policy issues, and reference was made to "the thanks of the Nation" that he had earned. Finally, wrote the President, "So I say: well done, in the hope that we can continue to call upon you for the counsel which you can give out of so rich and varied an experience."

Presidents and secretaries of state may be forgiven for playing down the unpleasantnesses and misunderstandings behind resignations and for playing up the accomplishments and the happy side of their relations. Probably it is done, however, less out of motives of magnanimity than for the purpose of hiding from the public policy clashes of the past, knowledge of which could weaken confidence in the administration. Actually, Secretary Byrnes, while attending a Council of Foreign Ministers in Moscow, had not kept the President informed of developments. Nor had he stood up to the Russians as much as the President had wished, for Truman had become "tired of babying the Soviets." Then, on arriving back in the United States, the Secretary had released a communique before conferring with his chief. On January 5, 1946, the President called Byrnes in and read a prepared letter explaining that he had not been informed about the proceedings of the Moscow Conference and that in any case he did not like the way in which things were going with Russia. The letter was a forthright and unequivocal denunciation of his Secretary's conduct. Although it did not ask for a note of resignation, its content and tone displayed so much Presidential disapproved that the Secretary of State could not fail to take the hint. Byrnes continued in office for several months, but on April 16 he penned his resignation. He would have done so earlier, no doubt, had he not been in the midst of important negotiations.

Just how serious any discord between the president and his secretary of state might be allowed to become before the latter should resign cannot be reduced to a simple formula. It depends on too many variables: the temperament of the two men; their mood of the moment; and the probable disturbance to the conduct of foreign affairs which an immediate change at the Department of State might entail. Byrnes delayed resigning for several months for the sake of what seemed to him to be the national interest. Bryan showed no haste when he got out, perhaps hoping that he could convert President Wilson and the Cabinet to his views; he was not, however, so slow as to become a serious handicap or a worry to his chief. Secretary Lansing has been criticized for differing so long and so sharply with President Wilson over problems of the peace settlement in 1919-1920 and not stepping down from his office before being asked to do so. How a secretary can hope to be of much use to his president when differences have become as acute and personal relations as strained as those between Lansing and Wilson is difficult to understand.

Resignations have on occasions been sudden and unforeseen as, for example, when Secretary McLane left President Jackson's Cabinet on June 30, 1834. It had been known that the two had been at odds on the question of rechartering the Bank of the United States, and rumors of resignation had circulated earlier; but at the time when the resignation actually came the public was not expecting it. Differences had been accumulating, and, when Jackson appointed Roger Taney to a position which McLane had sought on the Supreme Court bench, a parting of ways had been reached.

Quite unusual was the resignation of James G. Blaine in 1892. It came suddenly on June 4 in the form of a brief note which offered no explanation, no word of regret, and no reference to the personal relationship between him and President Harrison. The note was as follows:

> *June 4, 1892*
>
> To the President:
>
> I respectfully beg leave to submit my resignation of the office of Secretary of State of the United States to which I was appointed by you the 5th of March, 1889.
>
> The conditions of public business in the Department justifies me in requesting that my resignation be accepted immediately. I have the honor to be
>
> Very respectfully
> Your obedient servant
> *James G. Blaine*

The reply of the President was equally formal and chilly. Generally, unless things have been quite intolerable, the exchange of letters between a retiring secretary and his president is warm and friendly, as in the case of Secretary Brynes and President Truman. Probably no one will ever be completely sure of what was in the mind of Secretary Blaine when he wrote his brief note. Circumstantial evidence points to the fact that Blaine's deteriorating health was one explanation of his note; only shortly before he had left a Cabinet meeting early because he had not been well. Apparently, however, he had recovered from this particular complaint, and, in any case, ill health could hardly justify a terse, cold note like the one Blaine sent. The fact that Blaine and Harrison had never displayed any cordiality in their relations with each other was also known. There had been rumors of jealousy on the part of the President toward the Secretary for his high standing in the nation. Well understood was the President's desire to assert himself in foreign affairs and to leave little to the discretion of his Secretary. Some believed that Blaine never completely forgot the refusal by his chief to appoint the Secretary's son to the post of assistant secretary in the Department. A fair guess is that all of these considerations entered into the strange exchange between the two men in early June of 1892. Blaine's death, about six months after his resignation, lends weight to the contention that ill health was important among the several considerations in his decision to quit. That his method of leaving office displayed no warmth of feeling for the President simply reflected what was obvious—the men were not on good terms.

The lure of another position has been behind the resignations of several secretaries. John Jay, who had been our Secretary under the Articles of Confederation, resigned in 1789 to become Chief Justice of the Supreme Court; nevertheless he remained in charge of the State Department until Thomas Jefferson was ready to go to work on March 22, 1790. John Marshall left the Department for the same reason on February 4, 1801, and became the nation's most celebrated Chief Justice. Like Jay, he also continued for a while, until March 4, to act as Secretary of State, this time *ad interim*. Among the several reasons for the resignation of Secretary Root, on January 27, 1909, was the fact that he had just been elected United States Senator by the New York legislature. President-elect Taft urged Secretary Root to remain in the Department after his inauguration, but without avail. Indeed, the Secretary asked to be relieved even before the inauguration. His resignation in January led to the appointment of Robert Bacon, who served until the end of Taft's term.

Secretary John W. Foster left office under unusual circumstances on February 23, 1893, after only having served since the preceding June 29. At the time of his appointment he was preparing, for the Department of State, the case to be presented in the Bering Sea Arbitration with Great Britain. As Secretary, he continued with this task, which, together with the duties of his new office, kept him so busy that he had little time away from his desk, even in the evenings. Because he had prepared the case and understood it better than anyone else, he became the logical man to defend it before the tribunal. This, he believed, would divert him from the general work of the Department too much, and he therefore resigned. A situation of this kind would be unlikely to arise today, for the Department's activities are more refined and technicians more available, in matters of law as well as in other affairs.

For one reason or another, a secretary's wish to resign has often been thwarted or at least delayed by the president. Secretary Fish had reluctantly accepted office in the first place and wanted to retire as soon as it was possible to do so without embarrassing President Grant. Several times he offered to resign, but the President prevailed upon him to remain until the end of the long eight-year stretch. John Hay was never happy in office and would have been glad to be relieved but found no acceptable way out. He was so piqued by the action of the Senate on the first draft of the Hay-Pauncefote Treaty regarding an Isthmian canal that he sent in his resignation to President McKinley, but the President refused to accept it and assured him of White House support. Always impatient with the Senate, Hay said at this time, "When I sent in the

Canal Convention, I felt sure that no one out of a madhouse could fail to see that the advantages were all on our side." Again in 1903 he was on the point of leaving and suggested Elihu Root as a successor, but President Roosevelt dissuaded him. At the beginning of President Roosevelt's new term in 1905, he again made mild overtures toward quitting, this time because of his poor health.

Situations arise in which presidents feel justified in refusing to accept a resignation; continuity in the secretary's office is, of course, always an advantage both to the president and to the nation, provided the incumbent's work is satisfactory. It would be especially serious to lose the State Department head in the midst of a crisis or while he is engaged in important negotiations. Certainly a president can justify rejection of a resignation which has been offered by a secretary because of being victimized by a hostile senate or a critical public; President McKinley's refusal to accept Hay's offer of resignation following the Senate's adverse action on a treaty was good common sense. Wise presidents have had the foresight to prevent an attempt to resign by coming quickly to an embattled secretary's defense, as President Truman did for Acheson, and President Eisenhower for Dulles.

· IV

Policy Adviser to the President

In 1789 the Congress enacted a law setting up a Department of State, a law which is still in effect. In it the duties of the secretary of state are defined as follows:

> The Secretary of State shall perform such duties as shall from time to time be enjoined or entrusted to him by the President relative to correspondences, commissions, or instructions to or with public ministers or consuls from the United States, or to negotiations with public ministers from foreign states or princes, or to memorials or other applications from foreign public ministers or other foreigners, or to such other matters respecting foreign affairs as the President of the United States shall assign to the department, and he shall conduct the business of the department in such manner as the President shall direct.

This statute clearly makes the secretary of state the president's principal assistant in foreign affairs, to do whatever may be requested of him. The chief executive may rely on him only a little or heavily, making him anything from a first-class clerk to the administration's policy-maker. What actually happens depends on who the president is, who the secretary is, and the circumstances in which they are working together. In any case, they must have some kind of an understanding, assumed or specifically agreed upon, as to the role of each. In accordance with the president's wishes, the consultations which must occur between the two men on foreign affairs may be occasional or frequent; advice on a policy project may or may not be sought by the president; and advice given may be followed or ignored. Presidents may employ secretaries to negotiate treaties or agreements and to represent them in conferences and meetings if they so desire; on the other hand, they may do these tasks themselves, or make use of ambassadors and special agents.

Although this personal element in government is always prominent, nowhere does it stand out in bolder relief than here. All governmental posts, from that of the president to a town clerk, are shaped by the men occupying them fully as much as by the law creating them. But in the secretaryship of state two personalities rather than one come actively into play. In 1862, the office was fashioned by the personalities of Abraham Lincoln and William Seward. Under Theodore Roosevelt and John Hay in 1901, it was as different from what it had been in 1862 as the personalities of Roosevelt and Hay differed from those of Lincoln and Seward. The Eisenhower-Dulles team bore little resemblance to the Truman-Acheson combination.

An effort has sometimes been made by a president and his secretary at the beginning of their work to agree on the principles that should guide their joint efforts. Reference has already been made to the attempt of Cordell Hull before assuming office to have an understanding with President-elect Roosevelt. Said Hull, "I do not have in mind the mere carrying on of correspondence with foreign governments"; he felt that it should be his duty "to aid the President in every possible way in the formulation and conduct of foreign policy." Although the President-elect agreed to this role for his Secretary and, in fact, gave Hull a fairly free hand at first, later, when Hitler's aggressions made foreign affairs the prime issue of the hour, the chief executive began to manage things himself and to reduce Hull's policy-making role considerably.

The rub of personalities and the exigencies of the occasion, much more than any prior discussions or general principles, map the areas in which a given president and his secretary operate. This was true of President Roosevelt and Secretary Hull. The Secretary himself brought out in his *Memoirs* that, until 1936, domestic problems, the depression in particular, took nearly all of the President's attention; at the beginning of the President's second term, however, "his interest and participation in foreign affairs greatly increased." Hull nevertheless felt that his chief never reduced him to "a mere transmitter and receiver of messages to and from foreign governments." He explained that Roosevelt always sought his advice or concurrence before taking an important step, except in conferences with Mr. Churchill and Generalissimo Stalin, where military questions usually dominated. According to the Secretary, "Records on file in the State Department include numerous recommendations of policy from me to President Roosevelt; recommendations regarding steps to be taken; outlines with elaborate data for the foreign affairs portion of the President's public statements and addresses. . . ."

Despite Hull's explanations and protestations, his role in foreign affairs was for the most part a subordinate one. Even during his first four-year term, the President on one occasion asserted himself vigorously, much to the chagrin of his Secretary, and that was during the London Economic Conference of 1933 when his interference in proceedings fatally defeated Hull's plans. From 1936 on, major statements of policy emanated from the President. The famous "Quarantine" speech by Roosevelt in 1937 contained words and phrases not included in the preliminary draft examined by the Secretary. The President even bypassed the Department of State by dispatching Harry Hopkins on important missions abroad, thereby infuriating the Secretary. Hull was indignant, too, that he was not included in meetings with Churchill and Stalin. Generally, on the broad matter of policy, the chief executive came to be "his own secretary of state." What saved Hull's equanimity was that on most issues of policy he saw eye to eye with the President and did not feel that his own principles of conduct had been compromised.

Over our history, the relationships between the presidents and their secretaries have been of three main types: (1) the president dominant; (2) the secretary dominant; and (3) the two participating about equally, with neither one obviously in the ascendancy. The first President was inclined to be his own secretary of state, and his first appointee, Thomas Jefferson, cooperated with him on this basis. Washington made his own decisions, although he consulted Jefferson and also his Secretary of the Treasury, Alexander Hamilton. While he was constitutionally correct in relying heavily on Hamilton, the practice was complicating and unwise. It irritated not only Jefferson but also Edmund Randolph and Timothy Pickering, the next two incumbents at the State Department. This may well have been a factor in Jefferson's resignation, for he was constantly frustrated by Hamilton's opposition.

On one occasion, Secretary of State Jefferson dispatched a pointed note to British Minister Hammond defending the nonpayment by the states of their debts and their refusal to compensate Loyalists for losses incurred during the Revolution. Hamilton, who was pro-British, countered this by telling Hammond that Jefferson's note did not fairly represent the point of view of the Washington Administration. Both openly and in secret Hamilton dealt with Hammond, much as though he were in charge of foreign affairs. Such a practice would not be tolerated today by a president, as shown in 1946, when Secretary of Commerce Henry Wallace publicly denounced the policy pursued by Secretary of State Byrnes as being too friendly to Britain and too harsh to Russia. After protests by Byrnes and wide criticism by others had been registered, President Truman asked for the resignation of Secretary Wallace, stating, "The Government of the United States must stand as a unit in its relations with the rest of the world. . . ." President Washington's failure to support his Secretary of State against Hamilton and his frequent reliance on the Secretary of the Treasury in foreign policy revealed a lack of sophistication in politics. It was not surprising that the President encountered difficulty finding a man willing to take the appointment after Jefferson and Randolph had put up with such treatment and Randolph had left office under charges of intriguing with France.

The personality of a secretary of state has on occasions doomed him to domination by a more strong-willed president. Any observer of politics in 1809 might easily have foretold that Robert Smith, serving under a man of the caliber and experience of James Madison, would be relegated to an inferior place. Similarly, the appointment years later of aged Lewis Cass by President Buchanan showed unmistakably that the Chief Executive intended to direct policy. President McKinley's selection of John Sherman, also old and declining, was certain proof that the Secretary would not dominate. But, instead of creating a presidential monopoly in this case, it led the President to seek advice from Assistant Secretary Day.

Strong-minded presidents, bent upon running foreign affairs themselves, frequently discovered iron in the intellectual equipment of their secretaries. The result was inevitable—clash and frequently the resignation of the secretary, yielding the right of way to the chief executive. President Wilson, a man of convictions, found in his first two appointees, William Jennings Bryan and Robert Lansing, men as sure of themselves as he. In the early part of Wilson's administration there was a happy coincidence of views between the President and Secretary Bryan on all important issues. What finally tore them apart was controversy over the manner in which the United States should ply its course as a neutral in World War I. Bryan thought his own views on the subject more neutral than those of the President, and in the nonlegal sense they were, for he was intent more upon keeping out of war and concerned less with the niceties of the law of neutrality. From the beginning of the War, he was the only Cabinet member who did not have pro-ally leanings; consequently, he was destined to be a minority of one in many discussions. More specifically, Bryan was critical of his chief for taking so strong a stand in the *Lusitania* affair; he found Wilson's notes to Germany too harsh; he thought that British violations of American neutrality called for protests fully as severe as those made to Germany; and he demanded that American citizens be restricted in their travel abroad. The Secretary was miffed, too, when the President sent Colonel House instead of himself as a personal emissary to the belligerent capitals on a peace mission.

The determined mind of President Wilson collided with another immovable Secretary of State, Robert Lansing. The issues were many. Lansing saw in the German threat a danger to democracy everywhere, even to the United States, and was not wholly sympathetic with the President's effort to keep the nation out of war. He was critical of Wilson's decision to head the American delegation to the Paris Peace Conference and of the manner in which the delegates were chosen. He was disturbed by the attention Colonel House received at Paris, and he differed with the President on vital issues of the peace, including his estimate of the importance of a League of Nations. The boiling point was reached when, during the President's illness, Lansing called Cabinet meetings. He was soundly berated for this "assumption of Presidential authority" and asked to resign forthwith. Unlike Bryan's political demise, Lansing's was complicated by personal animosities.

In Bryan as well as in Lansing, President Wilson would have been well satisfied with somebody willing to do routine chores, but both had higher ambitions. For this reason, the position was a difficult one for both men. Referring to Lansing, Colonel House wrote in 1928, "No other Secretary of State had so difficult a task." There is, indeed, something incongruous in a presidential choice of a man with ideas to head the Department of State when the chief executive is altogether content with his own.

A more recent clash of this nature erupted between President Truman and Secretary Byrnes, when, as explained earlier, the Chief Executive held his man to account for not keeping him informed and for "babying the Soviets." Truman was determined to keep a firm hold on foreign affairs, and his concept of the secretary's job was one fully recognizing his own right to do so. In his *Memoirs*, he said, "Secretary of State should never have the illusion that he is President of the United States. Some Secretaries of State have had such illusions, but they would never admit it." He further explained that it is the secretary's business to advise, but that the chief executive cannot allow his secretary to make "basic decisions."

A president who wishes to manage foreign affairs himself has often found it advantageous to send a special agent abroad to convey a point of view to another government, to negotiate, or to get information. Not all special agents, however, have represented an effort to side-step the secretary, and many have been appointed with his approval, as in 1847, when Nicholas Trist was sent by President Polk to Mexico, with Secretary Buchanan's consent, to negotiate a peace settlement. At that time, the Department had no minister in Mexico to carry forward the work, and consequently there was no alternative procedure.

During World War I, President Wilson's employment of Colonel House on special missions in Europe was quite another thing, and it irritated both Secretary Bryan and Secretary Lansing. A careful student of the Department of State, Professor Graham Stuart, expressed the situation bluntly: "Colonel House, a close friend of the President's, ultimately came to play a more important role in the formulation of foreign policy than the Department of State." House conducted for some time all important negotiations with the Latin American diplomats. He traveled in Europe trying to negotiate an end to the war, and he reported back to Wilson directly on his observations and activities. Earl Grey, British Foreign Minister, said that, in his experience, affairs were often handled by the President without consulting the Secretary and by means of direct contact through Colonel House. This practice was continued throughout Secretary Lansing's tenure; House was a delegate to the Paris Peace Conference, and more meetings were held in his rooms than in Secretary Lansing's quarters.

Mrs. Bryan, writing about her husband's experiences, reported that the operations of Colonel House made the work of the Secretary "extraordinarily difficult." Secretary Lansing never filed a formal protest to the President, although he was greatly annoyed. Colonel House himself recognized the situation for what it was, saying, "My position was unusual and without precedent, and it would have been natural for him (Lansing) to object to my ventures in his field of activity." Any secretary will smart under these presidential slaps, but there is little he can do about it unless he is willing to go to the length of resigning. From the president's point of view, the practice is an effective means of keeping the major issues of policy closely under his own personal control.

Secretary Hull passed through the same torment during World War II. President Roosevelt saw fit to send a number of men abroad as his personal representatives on special missions; in addition to Harry Hopkins, the most conspicuous of them all, there were William Donovan, Henry Wallace, W. Averell Harriman, Myron Taylor, and Patrick Hurley. Harry Hopkins' work on Lend Lease related to food, fuel, shipping, and other interests which cut deeply into the business of diplomacy. It made him, in the words of Robert Sherwood, "Roosevelt's own personal foreign office." When Averell Harriman was in London as Lend Lease Expediter, with the rank of minister, he was housed in the Embassy but was essentially independent of it and reported directly to Hopkins. All of this was irritating to Secretary Hull, and relations between him and Hopkins were not cordial. In dealing with the State Department, Hopkins preferred to be in contact with Under Secretary Welles. Just what Roosevelt's motives were in by-passing the Department of State may only be surmised. It is possible, as John Gunther has said, that the President lost patience with Hull's "fussiness, slowness of grasp, and mountaineer conservatism" but kept him at the State Department because of his strong influence in the Senate. In any case, Hull was repeatedly ignored on important foreign policy matters or given no more than a perfunctory part. Roosevelt was, to quote John Gunther again, "his own Secretary of State—or Hopkins was."

Presidential domination at the expense of the secretary can be augmented by recourse to the cabinet in policy problems. If and when the chief executive so wishes, problems may be placed before the full cabinet for discussion and an expression of opinion. The earlier presidents were more inclined to follow this practice than recent ones; President Washington leaned heavily on his Cabinet. Because it deals with the military phases of policy, the National Security Council today rates well above the cabinet as an advisory body. Indeed it is often the real maker of policy, although in a technical sense it is merely advisory. The membership of the secretary of state in the Council ensures him of an opportunity to voice his views and thus to avoid being overlooked, but it does not guarantee that his opinions will win out. The secrecy of Council meetings precludes our knowing just how well a given secretary has fared in this respect. Early in his administration, President Kennedy consulted his White House Staff as well as his Secretary and the Security Council on policy problems.

Secretaries of state who belong to the second category mentioned earlier—those who have dominated foreign policy—were usually men of force serving either under weak presidents or under presidents who lacked the time to give their attention to external affairs. Under President Tyler, Secretary Daniel Webster was active and strong to a degree that few of his predecessors could equal. President Tyler was so busy trying to maintain harmony with his fellow Whigs that he could spare only a minimum of time for foreign problems. Moreover, in Webster he had a man fully capable of shouldering responsibility. Tyler was by no means a weakling, but he did find it convenient to place confidence in his reliable Secretary, offering advice, suggestions, and encouragement at times but without getting implicated any more than necessary in either the details or the broad outlines of policy. He left Webster free in negotiating the famous Webster-Ashburton Treaty with England; when negotiations seemed deadlocked, he called in Minister Ashburton and gave encouragement to a continuance of diplomatic effort, an act which Webster acknowledged with gratitude.

During the Civil War, President Lincoln found in Secretary of State Seward a strong right arm at a time when the gravest of all domestic problems kept the Chief Executive preoccupied. Frederic W. Seward, son of the Secretary, has recalled that on the first Sunday after his arrival in Washington, Lincoln told the senior Seward on the way home from church, "Governor Seward, there is one part of my work that I shall have to leave largely to you. I shall have to depend upon you for taking care of those little matters of foreign affairs, of which I know so little and with which I reckon you are familiar." The son records that Lincoln gradually reached the point where he signed papers from the Department of State without reading them. Certainly Seward was the moving force in such important matters as standing for American rights against neutral England and opposing French intrigues in Mexico.

In Charles Evans Hughes, President Harding had a Secretary of State with an aptitude well above his own for foreign affairs. On February 19, 1921, the President introduced Hughes to the press as his new Secretary and said, "From this time on, gentlemen, you will get your news as to the foreign relations of the United States from the State Department." Harding was glad to wash his hands of the whole sticky business and let his Secretary take the initiative in the Washington Disarmament Conference, the nonrecognition of Russia, Far Eastern problems, and Latin American affairs. According to current gossip, the President once asked a senator how he was going to vote on a treaty then pending in the Senate; when the senator replied that he had not read the treaty, Harding commented, "You haven't got anything on me; I haven't read it either." President Coolidge continued the Harding practice of relying on Secretary Hughes, but, when Frank Kellogg went to the Department in 1925, the Chief Executive began taking a stronger interest in policy problems.

To John Foster Dulles fell the major role in American policy under President Eisenhower. The President had in his Secretary a dedicated man with a good background in diplomacy, a man in whom it was easy to place confidence. Then, when Eisenhower became ill and had to curtail his activities, more and more the control of affairs centered in Dulles. So pronounced was this trend that Walter Lippmann wondered in an editorial ". . . whether responsibility is not concentrated to an unworkable degree in the mind and conscience of one man." Mr. Lippmann was, however, less critical of the President for the "one-man" system than of the Secretary for trying to keep all the reins of control in his own hands rather than relying on others in the Department. The President always maintained a vital interest in foreign policy, consulting his Secretary constantly and addressing the public from time to time, but initiative, drive, and what amounted in fact to decision all emanated from Dulles rather than the President.

Occasionally, the concept of prime minister has been associated with the office of secretary of state. A few ambitious secretaries have thought of themselves as prime ministers and, with the indulgence of the president, may have been allowed more than the usual amount of authority, even spilling over into the field of domestic politics. In brief, a secretary would be, or try to be, the power behind the throne, with the president becoming a figurehead, who, like the British Queen, would reign but not govern.

The term "prime minister" applied to a secretary of state is confusing and misleading. A minister he is, to be sure, and in a chronological sense his Department was the first to have been created. In matters of ceremony and precedence, he is also first among his colleagues of the cabinet. Priority, too, is accorded him by law over the other cabinet members in succession to the presidency. Some few have been powerful, even in domestic affairs, but none has approached in status the Queen's prime minister in England. When a British newspaper referred to Secretary Dulles as Eisenhower's "Prime Minister," its editor must have misunderstood his actual position or meant that in foreign affairs alone he held primacy.

More than other secretaries, William Seward and James G. Blaine wanted to act as prime ministers and tried to control the chief executive in domestic as well as in foreign affairs. The two men were alike in that, when coming into office, they were better known and had a stronger party influence than the Presidents over them, Lincoln and Garfield; they were, therefore, strategically located to dominate the government. Both were ambitious and able men, fully capable of being prime ministers if, perchance, the opportunity fell their way. In *An Autobiography*, Charles Francis Adams wrote that Lincoln "was an absolutely unknown quantity; so much so that a little later, as subsequently appeared, Seward invited him practically to abdicate, delegating full authority to himself."

Lincoln never abdicated, nor did he come anywhere near it, but he did rely on his Secretary of State a great deal during the trying years of his tenure. Even before the inauguration ceremonies on March 4, 1861, the President-elect, far away in Illinois, kept in constant communication with Seward in Washington to find out what was going on and to get the opinions of the shrewd politician from New York. Just before the inauguration, Seward brushed up against his chief in a way that should have told him that Lincoln was not going to be a figurehead in the White House. When selecting his Cabinet, the President-elect included Chase over Seward's opposition; Seward withdrew his acceptance of the secretaryship of state in protest. Lincoln persuaded him to reconsider and after the inauguration had a long conversation with him in which reconciliation and the solidarity of the new administration were in some measure effected. Significant was the fact that the President-elect chose his Cabinet himself except for one post, as Gideon Welles has explained, and that Seward had only a small part in the process. This was not an auspicious beginning for a would-be prime minister, for in England prime ministers select their cabinets.

The wide range of Seward's activities as Secretary of State, wide enough to include domestic interests of many kinds, furnishes the principal reason for thinking of him as wielding more power than the usual incumbent. The President had a great deal of confidence in his Secretary, and the feeling became mutual as time passed. Seward often explained how busy he was, and, indeed, he could allude to a host of duties which kept him continually occupied. In the spring of 1861, he gave the following account of his routine: "I am counseling with the Cabinet one hour, with the Army officers the next, the Navy next, and I visit the troops as fast as they come. I dare not, because I cannot safely, leave this post from which all supplies, all directions, all inquiries must radiate. . . ." The President consulted with him on the issuance of the Emancipation Proclamation. He often acted as the President's agent in calling Cabinet meetings. Seward's intention to run the government came out in an early memorandum to Lincoln dated April 1, 1861, which he called "Some Thoughts for the President's Consideration." After reciting the things that needed to be done, he said that either the President must do them or turn them over to a Cabinet member and that, although the work was not his "especial province," he would "neither seek to evade or to assume responsibility." The numerous duties which he assumed kept him working long hours. With the solace of his well-known cigar, he often worked on Sunday, taking care of week-end mail from abroad. His high position was further brought out by his extensive entertaining, which included such groups as the Cabinet, the Diplomatic Corps, and even the Supreme Court.

So active was Seward in the affairs of government that he received much of the blame for the failures which harried the nation. Many people thought of him as meddlesome and inefficient. By December, 1862, when Congress convened, the feeling was so deep that Republican members adopted a resolution asking for Seward's resignation and presented it to the President. The Secretary offered to resign, but, showing the appreciation he felt for Seward's services, Lincoln refused to accept the resignation. Actually, Seward was too useful a man to the overburdened President and to the cause of the Union to be lost.

A few years after the Civil War, Charles Francis Adams, a friend of Seward, made an address in which he pictured the Secretary of State as the genius behind Lincoln, the real power in the government. In *Galaxy* magazine (1873), the Honorable Gideon Welles, a member of the Lincoln Cabinet, wrote a long and laborious article to show that Adams was wrong. He explained convincingly that "In the executive council and in measures of administration the Secretary had influence, not always happily exercised, but the President's was always the master mind." He admitted Seward's usefulness, despite mistakes, but insisted that the Secretary was "never the superior and controlling executive mind." The truth is now unmistakable: Lincoln was in fact as in name the Chief Executive, and Seward was his able helper whose influence and advice were respected but not necessarily followed. Seward was not a prime minister as that term is used abroad or in the sense that he transformed the President into a figurehead. Lincoln's ability to make his own decisions is illustrated by the well-known incident in a Cabinet meeting when a vote taken disclosed the whole group answering "no" to a proposal while his was the only "aye." Undaunted by the unanimous vote against him and aware of the purely advisory nature of a cabinet vote, Lincoln announced the results, "seven nays, one aye—the ayes have it." That Lincoln was no figurehead was implied in Seward's letter to his wife a few months after taking office, in which he wrote: "Executive force and vigor are rare qualities. The President is the best of us." Seward was Lincoln's first minister in usefulness and in importance, and he brought to the office of Secretary of State an unprecedented range of activities. But he did not have the general supervision over other departments characteristic of a prime minister, nor did he have the power of decisions. Unlike the advice of the British prime minister to the Queen, his advice to the President might be overruled.

Secretary James G. Blaine under President Garfield also pressed his office into the forefront. Indeed, his biographer, David Muzzey, refers to him as the President's "premier." He undoubtedly was Garfield's most prominent and most useful Cabinet member, and his advice extended to a multitude of issues, some outside the field of foreign affairs. The President leaned heavily upon him. The extent to which the Secretary took part in the selection of Garfield's Cabinet is not altogether clear. His opinions were sought and given but historians disagree on the extent to which they were adopted; some were convinced that certain appointees were named over Blaine's opposition. Blaine fitted comfortably into Garfield's conception of his duties, and, when, years later, he became President Harrison's Secretary of State, he was restless in the more restricted role assigned to him.

The advice of secretaries of state has sometimes been sought, if not followed, by newly elected presidents in the choice of other cabinet members. When this has happened, the office has assumed an importance outside the field of foreign affairs which might suggest the prime minister idea, even though the other attributes of the Queen's first minister were lacking. Secretaries Webster, Bryan, and Knox gave opinions to their respective presidents on filling other posts. Biographer Herbert Wright took special note of the influence of Secretary Knox with

President Taft in making up the Cabinet, together with his suggestions to the President on other matters. Wright concluded, ". . . Knox, in accepting the portfolio of foreign affairs, considered himself, and seemed to be considered, as a sort of prime minister in the new administration." The rumor that Knox considered resigning because his influence beyond the State Department had not been as great as he had expected may have been well founded. Knox and Taft were good friends, at least when they began working together, and the President admitted the large contributions of his Secretary of State in foreign policy. The self-importance of Knox and his overbearing attitude, however, did irk Taft, who understated the situation when he said, "There is no lack of confidence in Knox."

Several secretaries worked under two or more presidents and thus themselves discovered how closely the methods and quirks of the chief executive could affect their job. James G. Blaine served under three chief executives—Garfield, Arthur, and Harrison—but it was under Garfield and Harrison that the contrast between a president willing to be led and one determined to lead was most striking.

John Hay headed the State Department under President McKinley for two and one-half years and then continued for a little more than four years under President Roosevelt. Unlike McKinley, who had left policy problems with his Secretary, Theodore Roosevelt was determined to play an active part. Professor A. L. P. Dennis wrote of McKinley that his "horizon toward the foreign world was clouded by his actual ignorance of conditions and policies. . . . Let Hay manage matters of diplomacy! That seemed to be the attitude of President McKinley." The contrast between Hay's position under McKinley and that under Roosevelt was well stated by William Thayer: "Mr. Hay used to tell his friends that often President McKinley did not send for him once a month on business, but that he saw President Roosevelt every day. That statement illustrates the difference in initiative between the two presidents. . . ." The President's hand was often in evidence, as for instance in negotiations for the construction of the Panama Canal. It takes an exceptional man to be able to work successfully under presidents as unlike as the two in office when John Hay was Secretary of State.

Because the mode and extent of secretarial and presidential participation in policy-making are the products of a personal relationship between two men, there is much that no one can ever know about the fifty-three secretaries and thirty-four presidents. When the weight of one is well out of balance with the weight of the other, the public, with its flair for gossip, will be aware of the fact. But when there is an even give-and-take, few if any observers will notice it, unless by chance there is an angry exchange. Publicized or unpublicized, cooperating or scrapping, several secretaries have contributed on a somewhat equal basis with their respective presidents to the substance of policy; they, therefore, fall into the third group as earlier defined.

Both President Monroe and his Secretary of State, John Quincy Adams, were able, determined men, well versed in the diplomacy of their time. Both were active in American policy, and they cooperated reasonably well. It would be misleading and unfair to say that they contributed equally, but they did work closely together, neither assuming to act without the support of the other. Adams, determined to the point of obstinacy, won on most subjects of debate and for that reason probably shaped the course of our history more than did his chief. He stood out successfully against the whole Cabinet in support of General Jackson's ventures in Florida in opposition to Spain; he won his President over to a policy of delaying recognition of the new Latin American states; and he played a vital, if not the most vital, role in the formulation of the Monroe Doctrine. These battles were impersonal and friendly, with both men informed and active.

Between President Polk and Secretary of State Buchanan there was competition for power and control, without an open breach or deadlock, but with the result that both men played an active part in policy. Both had strong convictions and personally were not on the best of terms. In his diary, President Polk wrote, "Mr. Buchanan will find that I cannot be forced to act against my convictions and that if he chooses to retire, I will have no difficulty in administering the Government without his aid." When, in 1845, Polk withdrew an offer to Great Britain on the Oregon question, it appeared that he was asserting this boasted independence of spirit.

President Hoover and his Secretary, Henry L. Stimson, were both interested in foreign affairs, and were both capable men. At the beginning of his term of office, President Hoover asked his newly appointed head of the State Department to spend ten days with him at the White House so that the two could become better acquainted with each other. Each found much to admire in the other, despite strong temperamental differences. No one can say in their work together just what the contributions of each were to the common cause, but it seems probable that both men made important ones. They differed with each other frequently and argued, but from these differences came policies. They worked together on a national policy to be followed at the London Naval Conference of 1930 and at the Geneva Conference two years later. They agreed on a more friendly policy in Latin America, and it was President Hoover who originated the term "good neighbor," later adopted by President Roosevelt and used effectively. The two men differed somewhat on how to deal with the aggressions of Japan in 1931, the greatest problem of foreign policy faced by them. Stimson, a man of action, favored strong, collective measures by the nations interested in the Far East whereas the President was against sanctions of any kind, economic or military, and was satisfied with a policy of refusing to recognize any Japanese conquests. In the end this policy prevailed, with both men supporting it.

Not long after Christian Herter became Secretary, it became clear that the imbalance characteristic of the

Eisenhower-Dulles team no longer existed. Throughout his tenure of nearly two years, Herter took part in a number of important meetings, especially those of the foreign ministers. He negotiated, and he gained the confidence of men with whom he worked both at home and abroad; in an inconspicuous way he carried on creditably. But the President asserted more initiative than before and made more policy statements than he had when Dulles was in office. His extensive travels abroad also testified to his personal involvement in a larger way.

The partnership of secretary and president in foreign affairs will in the future, as in the past, be a pliant one in which the contributions of each will be defined by the rub of personality against personality. This is as it should be, for the personal factor in government, besides being ineradicable, is also a means to flexibility. Were it possible to build high fences around defined areas, one for the secretary and one for the president, within which each must confine himself, a deadening rigidity would follow. Ambiguities and uncertainties in government, although they may seem objectionable, actually serve the useful purpose of providing it with that bending quality which prevents a break under strain.

Whatever division of labor may be worked out between secretary and president, responsibility is not and cannot be divided; the Constitution lodges it irrevocably in the chief executive. He is accountable to the nation both for his own actions and for the doings of his secretary in foreign affairs. Unity at this point could not be lost without confusion to the public, which, in some easy way, must be able to fix blame for the mistakes of officials and to award credit for accomplishments. In the final analysis, it is this unity of responsibility which justifies the president in assigning to his secretary of state whatever role he pleases in policy-making.

The position of the secretary as policy adviser to the president has undergone important changes as other agencies than the State Department have been brought deeply into the management of foreign affairs. The complications of contemporary world politics are such that policy-making will frequently demand data and opinions more available outside the State Department than within it. On pressing questions of national security, the president needs the help of admirals and generals. Recognizing the economic underpinning necessary to foreign policy when dealing with such matters as foreign aid, communist economic warfare, trade, and Common Market problems, he will require ready access to the secretary of the treasury, the secretary of commerce, the budget director, and many other officials strategically placed in economic matters. He must have a clear channel open to officials dealing with propaganda abroad, international agricultural problems, civil defense, and many other interests. To meet the expanded needs of the chief executive for assistance, changes have been effected in the government which aim to provide him with more diversified sources of advice. Indeed, new agencies have been created which are so active that they seem on first glance to challenge the primacy of the State Department and its head in foreign policy. The National Security Council, the Central Intelligence Agency, and the Atomic Energy Commission today play vital roles in American foreign policy, which have affected the secretary of state's advisory functions significantly. Several administrative departments, especially the Defense Department, are also active in international affairs. The increased importance of agencies external to the State Department has not diminished the secretary's advisory role as might be expected, mainly because he works with most of them either as a member or as a cooperating outsider. They have more often changed than detracted from his work and its utility. Actually, he is more strategically located now than he was fifty years ago to advise the president, but he advises in cooperation with other agencies and departments.

The National Security Council is the agency which in recent years has had the spotlight in foreign policy. It was created by Congress in 1947 to advise the president in the strategic aspects of policy, which of course are the most vital of all and actually a phase of nearly everything that our government does abroad. In offering advice to the president, the Council is expected to bring into a sensible whole the domestic, foreign, and military aspects of national security. It must maintain a balance between our foreign commitments, our military capabilities, and our economic resources. The operations of the organ are facilitated by intelligence reports submitted to it by the Central Intelligence Agency, created by Congress in the same statute (1947) which set up the Council itself. The work of the CIA, although concerned principally with the acquisition and analysis of intelligence data, has also on occasion had a close relation to policy and included operating activities, as in Cuba (1961). In its work the Council is assisted by a Planning Board, composed of assistant secretaries from the departments and agencies represented on it; this Board prepares papers on the broad framework of policy which will be analyzed by the Council itself. When the Cuban crisis was at its height in October, 1962, the President met every morning with a committee of the Council.

The objective which the National Security Council embodies in bringing the points of view of specialists in several fields to bear on its work of advising the president is evident from its composition. Its statutory members are the president, vice-president, secretary of state, secretary of defense, and director of the office of Civil and Defense Mobilization. Other officials are invited to meetings; the secretary of the treasury and the director of the Budget Bureau attend regularly by invitation of the president, and others take part occasionally, as their presence is needed. The chairman of the Joint Chiefs of Staff and the director of the Central Intelligence Agency are statutory advisers of the Council.

The functioning of the National Security Council affects the advisory duties of the secretary of state in several ways. First, it means that he will do some of his advising in the Council where the chief executive sits as chairman, although the two men will also consult elsewhere whenever they wish to do so. Secretary Acheson has explained that "there were times when I would see the President on business almost every day, and rarely less than four times a week"; two of those meetings were in the Cabinet and the National Security Council. Assisted as he is in his thinking by meeting with other high officials in the Department of State and by the information and data which his Department supplies him, the secretary's contributions to Council deliberations should at least equal those of any other member. Second, from his presence in the Council the secretary may be expected to gain new perspectives on policy not available from his Department —economic, military, political, psychological, etc.—that will enhance his advisory capabilities. No one better than he, the only member of the Council who gives all his time to foreign affairs, should be able to analyze and synthesize the diverse points of view presented and work them over into sound policy advice for the president.

The secretary of state also maintains a close relationship with other departments and agencies whose operations take them into the foreign field: the Department of Agriculture on the Food for Peace Program, the work of the Food and Agriculture Organization, etc.; the Department of Commerce on reciprocal trade agreements; the Department of the Treasury on the International Bank and the International Monetary Fund; the Export-Import Bank; and many others. In the process of correlating the activities of these agencies with the major foreign policies of the government through interdepartmental committees and other means of consultation, the secretary again enriches his background as an adviser to the president.

As it has developed, then, instead of being lost or submerged in the modern advisory system to the president, the secretary of state has remained at its center. As ever, the president is free to rely on his secretary as much or as little as he pleases. The president may still "be his own secretary of state"; he may listen to other members of the

National Security Council more than to his secretary, he may use a Colonel House, or he may advise with his White House staff as President Kennedy has done, especially during the early part of his administration. But, as always, the secretary is available to the chief executive, and, more than ever before, his relationships with other governmental agencies enable him to offer advice of high quality. In policy-making he is less expendable than ever.

Although in major questions of policy the secretary of state is only an adviser, in minor matters he feels free to make decisions without consulting the president. Secretary Hull explained that he used his judgment as to whether a departmental question or a policy problem were sufficiently important to require presidential attention. If so, he would outline his views on the subject to his chief. If, however, "a question of policy was not important enough to be brought to his attention, or it fell sufficiently within a well-defined philosophy on which he had already entertained a favorable attitude," the Secretary dealt with it himself. This is the usual practice.

·V·

Head of a Department

Whether he likes it or not—and often he has thoroughly disliked it—the secretary of state is the administrative head of a government department. Under him are bureaus, offices, divisions, and human beings with a multitude of titles and duties. Some 7,000 men and women are employed in the Washington offices of the Department of State, while abroad 15,500 promote American interests in embassies, legations, and consulates. These 22,500 men and women, numerous enough to make up a small city, answer to the secretary for their work and conduct, or to somebody else who is accountable to him.

Like a large and growing family, the Department's mounting personnel has posed a tough housing problem. Secretary Jay quartered his half-dozen helpers in a small residence at 13 South Sixth Street in Philadelphia, from whence the Department was moved, with the rest of the government, first to New York and later to Washington, D. C. When Seward took over, it was located at the corner of Fifteenth Street and Pennsylvania Avenue, pressed for space in a building of between thirty and forty rooms. He took it to a building just completed and intended to be used as an orphan asylum. In 1875 Secretary Fish set up Departmental housekeeping in a new building at Seventeenth Street and Pennsylvania Avenue, constructed for joint use by the War, Navy, and State Departments and looked upon then as one of the world's finest office buildings. In 1947, one day after he was commissioned, Secretary Marshall began installing the Department, greatly enlarged during World War II, into new quarters at Twenty-first Street and Virginia Avenue, popularly called "Foggy Bottom," a term derived, so we are assured, not from its intellectual processes but from the prevailing condition of weather in the area.

Spacious though it was, Foggy Bottom of 1947 could not meet the needs of an expanding Department, and extra room had to be found in temporary annexes and other buildings. In 1956 plans were laid to enlarge the building with an enormous south facade which would include a new main entrance. Now Foggy Bottom, old and new together, is one of the largest structures in the District of Columbia, covering four city blocks, and is able to meet the needs of the entire Department. Building on the new project was begun on September 18, 1956, when Deputy Under Secretary Loy Henderson, in the presence of other high officials of the Department, wielded a wrecking bar to bring down the building sign on old Temporary Building H at the corner of Twenty-third and C Streets. Back in 1790 John Jay would have found it difficult even to imagine a future Department of State elegantly housed in a $60,000,000 structure.

The dependence of the secretary of state on his Department in every phase of his work would be hard to exaggerate. On it he must rely for most of his information on the conditions and problems abroad with which he must cope in formulating policy proposals and advice for the president, although he also has the benefit of the reports of the Central Intelligence Agency and his conferences with other officials. From American embassies and legations abroad a steady flow of information and suggestions comes into the Department of State, whose offices digest it and make it available to experts and officials dealing with policy. The secretary must lean on his subordinates for information and help when he prepares to negotiate with the diplomats of other nations. Negotiations can never be successful unless they are prepared in advance so that there is an understanding of the position of the other party—how willing it may be to make concessions, what concessions we can safely make, and the arguments (supported by reliable data) that our side will advance. The secretary needs the assistance of his Department in his relations with Congress, at times to speak for him before its committees or to consult with its members, and on other occasions to give him the briefing that will enable him to perform such tasks himself. He cannot himself undertake more than a small fraction of the work of maintaining good relations with the American public—informing the people, answering letters, issuing passports, etc. To subordinates must be assigned the job of managing the foreign service which promotes our interests abroad in countless ways. There are documents to publish, communications to translate, a departmental budget to prepare, research to be done, contacts with the United Nations and other international organizations to maintain, and a long list of other chores. A strong Department will lend strength and wisdom to the secretary in all that he himself does and in those activities delegated to others for which he is held responsible.

As the secretary of state is dependent on the Department in all that he does, so the Department is dependent on its secretary. An observer of the operations of its bureaus, offices, and divisions must be impressed by the extent of their routine activities, many of which have little or no relationship to foreign policy, although in some way they serve American interests. He will find officials working over diplomatic correspondence for publication in *Foreign Relations of the United States*, others maintaining contact with universities to procure candidates for the foreign service, and still others translating documents. The range of activities, like that within an army, covers much besides the primary function of the organization. Without a head the Department would lack unity and integration; it would move without purpose and direction. For the proper execution of the Department's operational functions, therefore, as well as for the aid which the secretary can get in policy matters from subordinate officials, there is inevitably an administrative side to his routine.

This close tie between the secretary and his Department brings no assurance that he will take an active interest in organizational details. The early secretaries had such a small number of subordinates that problems of departmental management were few, even negligible; this was true of Secretary Madison who, after a tenure of eight years, left the Department substantially as he had found it. Some were lucky enough to inherit an efficient organization from their predecessors and felt no need to improve it; Secretary Evarts took office right after Secretary Fish had given the Department a good overhauling and was therefore free from such worries. Others have neglected organizational matters simply because they preferred not to be bothered by them. John Hay was not interested in routine; consequently, few changes were made during his seven years of service. He added some few minor offices such as an assistant solicitor, a translator, a law clerk, and a passport bureau, but he did not consider major changes.

Reorganization projects have many times been stalled by a Congress unwilling to enact the statutes or to provide the money required. Within their allotted budgets, however, secretaries have had a fair latitude of authority for reform without going to Capitol Hill. Secretary McLane included in his reorganization plans an item that would increase the annual salary of his chief clerk from $2,500 to $3,000. In 1834 he sent a note in which he requested the increase to the House Ways and Means Committee, pointing out that the official was "in fact, though not in name, an assistant or undersecretary" and that the duties of the office required not only "great fidelity, but talent and education of a high order. . . ." The Congress did not agree and refused the money. Although a secretary may bear the disappointment in so small a matter without too much frustration, he can be seriously handicapped when his major proposals fall under the axe of Congress. When the budget of the Department was cut $4,500,000 in 1933, as a depression measure, personnel problems multiplied.

To come into the office of secretary of state and find departmental affairs in a chaotic state has not been unusual. Secretary John Q. Adams discovered to his dismay that no filing system had been kept and that copies of letters and documents could not be found. Referring to this situation, he said in his *Memoirs*, "All is disorder and confusion." He worked out new methods for handling correspondence so that he would know where to find it and be able to use it. Continuing his campaign, he issued an executive order defining specifically the duties and the salaries of clerks. Adams reorganized the Department's library, which had had little attention, installing it in two rooms of the new building occupied in 1820. By these and other changes, which may appear to us of minor importance in these days of more pressing problems, the Secretary equipped the Department to keep up with the increasing pace of business.

The first overall reorganization of the Department was made by Secretary McLane in an executive order of 1833. The need was so urgent that President Jackson, in 1829, had mentioned in a message to Congress "the importance of so organizing that Department so that its Secretary may devote more of his time to our foreign relations." A number of bureaus were created and clerks assigned to each of them: diplomatic bureau; consular bureau; home bureau; bureau of archives, laws and commissions; bureau for pardons and remissions and copyrights and for the care of the library; disbursing and superintending bureau; and translating and miscellaneous bureau. The project embodied a new distribution of duties and responsibilities.

Such mistakes as came out in subsequent practice were eliminated by later orders.

When he became Secretary of State in 1845, Buchanan faced organizational problems which had been accumulating for years. In a report to the Judiciary Committee of the House of Representatives he disclosed that all of our diplomatic correspondence, which by this time had become voluminous, was carried on by three regular clerks and two copying clerks. He brought out, too, that he was the only person in the Department able to sign papers of any kind or to make decisions. In short, he was swamped with the details of his office, so that, as he asserted, "He must either neglect the national interests or the subordinate but primary business involving the rights of individuals. . . ." He felt that he did not have the time he needed to read and keep informed on his work. Freeing the secretary from the burden of details incidental to every administrative department has remained one of the basic objectives of reorganization projects.

Among those secretaries who have struggled most with reorganization problems have been Louis McLane, Hamilton Fish, Philander Knox, and Edward Stettinius, Jr., although others have worked at it and made changes of one kind or another. Hamilton Fish, like many other secretaries, was caught up in one of those economy drives in Congress which, strangely enough, always hit the Department of State hard, as though the conduct of foreign relations were a luxury easily dispensed with. Congress cut the number of his clerks from forty-eight to thirty-one for the year beginning on July 1, 1869. Six months later, Fish took the offensive and asked Congress for a new solicitor of claims and three more clerks. He needed clerical help, so he said, to index documents and papers which had been so badly handled that he had to rely on the memories of older members of his staff like Assistant Secretary Hunter for information. William Hunter, Jr. was one of the most distinguished public servants the Department has had during its history, and, if it were necessary to rely on anybody, he would be a good selection. But relying on memories is always hazardous and quite unnecessary when infallible records can readily be made available. From this point on, getting help from Congress, Fish set to work on a thorough reorganization plan for his Department, which allocated business among nine bureaus, two agencies, a translator, and a telegraph operator.

Although from the standpoint of policy, Philander Knox would not qualify as a great Secretary, his work in the area of Departmental organization would, as Graham Stuart has stated, "surely rate among the top half dozen." Knox may have been lazy, as President Taft once said, but he did not show it in the way he went about the task of reforming the Department. Huntington Wilson, who helped Knox, had a high regard for the Secretary's ability in administrative matters. Many innovations were introduced, not least of which was the establishment of three new geographical divisions—Western European, Near Eastern, and Latin American; one such division on Far Eastern affairs was already in existence.

During Secretary Hull's tenure, the need for organizational reform grew more and more imperative. The size of the Department had mushroomed in response to wartime conditions, but Hull had no time to give to the problem, nor had he any inclination to grapple with it. When Edward Stettinius, Jr. was made Under Secretary of State, it was understood that one of his major jobs would be to work out reorganization plans. He applied to the task his extensive business experience, but without the advantage of an understanding of the intricacies of diplomacy. His work was made difficult by Hull's trip to Moscow and his obligation to perform as Acting Secretary for a considerable period of time, but gradually plans were put together. The first executive order embodying them was issued on January 15, 1944, while Hull was still Secretary, and the last one went out on December 20, after Stettinius had been the head of the Department for three weeks. Most significant among the many changes made was the creation of the Office of Public Information, which not only absorbed the old divisions dealing with current information, research, and publication, but also added a new division for motion pictures and radio and another for science, education, and art. The Stettinius reorganization was by no means perfect, but it was constructive.

Because he felt the need for a better system of contact between himself and the functioning of the Department, General Marshall as Secretary of State created an Executive Secretariat, which has proved to be useful. This agency has many duties, most important of which is to direct and control "the orderly and prompt flow of official action and information documents to and from the secretary . . . assuring full correlation of relevant responsibilities in the preparation of policy recommendations," as the Department's Manual of Operations asserts. The Secretariat also sees that the decisions and requests of the secretary are implemented. As Mr. Henry Wriston has described the office, it is the "staff arm" of the secretary, making the Department a much more available and effective instrument of assistance to the secretary in all his work and especially in his advice to the president on policy-making.

Secretary Marshall brought to the Department another innovation designed to strengthen its usefulness to its head as an adviser on policy to the president when he set up a Policy Planning Staff. It is a small group of ten or twelve persons, serving at the pleasure of the secretary, created to look at policy from a broad perspective, to recognize emerging problems at an early stage, to consider the shape which policy should take from a long-range point of view, and to be critical of present policies. Although the usefulness of the Staff is conceded, it has often been criticized for its absorption with current policy problems and its consequent failure to do what has been expected of it in long-range planning.

Mr. Robert R. Bowie has called attention to two procedures by which recent secretaries of state have sought to maintain such a working relationship with the Department as to derive from it a maximum amount of help in his work, advisory and otherwise. One, followed by Secretary Marshall, has been to delegate to the Under Secretary "authority over policy formulation, operations, and administration"; the Under Secretary, working with subordinates, defined issues and placed problems before the Secretary for decision, always "with a written analysis and recommendation." A second procedure, followed by Secretaries Acheson and Dulles, has been to meet with senior officials of the Department "for discussion regarding issues and proposals." Whereas Mr. Acheson prepared such meetings by having groups of officials study in advance the problems to be taken up, Mr. Dulles circulated proposals among interested officials.

By these processes the skill and wisdom within the Department of State can be applied to policy projects and passed on to its head, who, after analyzing and working them over himself, is better equipped to advise the president. In crises and emergencies, short cuts will, of course, be taken in order to hasten the decision-making process. Without the assistance of subordinates in the Department, the advice of the secretary to the president could be nothing more than a personal opinion. With that assistance and the help he gets from other contacts, it becomes an opinion based on the information, experience, analysis, and deliberation of a group of men whose business it is to be in close touch with assigned phases of current problems.

Although the secretary of state, as head of the Department, is responsible for its proper organization and maintenance, for requests that Congress effect desired changes in the law on its structure, and for the submission of budgetary proposals for its support, in fact he no longer has the time to give these matters much attention. Fifty years ago Secretary Knox could and did spend a great deal of time on details. Now a secretary is too occupied with policy problems to be able to do so, and, unless he has some special projects of Departmental improvement, as did Secretary Marshall, he is usually satisfied to leave administrative affairs to other top-level officials under his direction. His tendency is, as Mr. Henry Wriston has said, "to eschew administration." Unless an under secretary and other officials are kept at work maintaining the organization and administration of the Department at a high point of efficiency, its deterioration could be a serious matter, handicapping the secretary in all that he does.

Power to appoint high officials in the Department, the ambassadors and the ministers, belongs, under the Constitution, to the president, acting with the consent of the Senate. Legally he is free to submit nominees to the Senate without consulting his secretary of state; but, in practice, presidents have often, although certainly not always, relied on help from their secretaries. Feeling, and not without reason, that no one's work will be more affected than theirs by the quality of the selections, some secretaries have sought a part in the process. Their weapon, if they care to use one for the purpose, can be quite effective—threat of resignation. Secretary Fish used it against President Grant shortly after the new administration went into office early in 1869. Grant was making a rather clean sweep in diplomatic posts, retaining only five of thirty-five ministers, and he was sponsoring a number of appointments which seemed bad to Fish. The Secretary protested the appointment of General M. C. Meigs, who had been doing a good job as Quartermaster General, to the post of Minister to Moscow. Apparently, Meigs was appointed in order to create an opening in the army for one of Grant's wartime friends. A little later, when the President was about to make three diplomatic appointments which seemed discreditable, Fish sent in his resignation. The stratagem worked, and Grant, anxious to keep his Secretary, agreed to ignore all outside pressures in his selections. Thereupon, Fish withdrew his resignation and renewed his efforts to raise the level of diplomatic appointments. He succeeded in placing some able men in office, including George Boker to Moscow and John W. Foster to Mexico. But resignation or threat of resignation may be a dangerous as well as an effective weapon, for what if the president were to accept it!

As Secretary of State, Martin Van Buren became incensed at President Jackson's independent action in making appointments and objected to his selections. Even before Van Buren had sat down at his office desk, Jackson had named ministers to London and Paris. The Secretary was able to handle the situation. As their administrative superior, he insisted that the two men leave for their posts at an early date, a demand which he knew they could not meet, and he thereby secured their resignations. From that time on the President was attentive to his Secretary's wishes when appointments were to be made.

John Hay had little to do with appointments under President McKinley, but he appeared unperturbed, even happy, that he did not have to deal with office seekers. His close friend, Whitelaw Reid, in the fall of 1898 asked him for the post of ambassador to London. Replying on November 13, Hay wrote to his friend in a facetious vein, "As to appointments under the State Department it is clear that I am to have nothing to say. I could not appoint even my Private Secretary, as Mr. Sherman wanted me to appoint his; nor my confidential clerk, as a friend of the President's from Canton had the place." A little later, Hay wrote to Reid: "My wishes will cut no figure. The President will do what seems to him best." It was a matter of some embarrassment to Hay to turn down his friend's request. Finally, the London appointment went to Joseph H. Choate.

When he became Secretary of State under President Coolidge in 1925, Frank Kellogg sponsored Dwight Morrow as his Under Secretary, although by that time a tradition had been fairly well established that the office should be given to a man of wide experience in diplomacy. Mr. Morrow had had no such experience; he had been a banker of the House of Morgan. The appointment would have ousted from the position no less a diplomat than Joseph C. Grew, who for twenty years had held different posts in the Department. The President considered the proposal and finally remarked, "No, I don't think that would do." Grew was retained in the office, and the Department was stronger because of his presence. Coolidge did, however, appoint Robert Olds, a friend and law partner of Kellogg, to the position of Assistant Secretary of State.

President Roosevelt consulted Secretary Hull in appointments, as is usual, but, as is also usual, the President's word was final. Hull has explained that, before he was commissioned, Roosevelt had suggested William Phillips as Under Secretary, and Hull had acquiesced. The President, on his own, named Raymond Moley as an Assistant Secretary, a selection which displeased the Secretary. Roosevelt and Hull worked together on the appointment of ambassadors; at times suggestions emanated from the White House but more often from the Department. The Secretary was piqued that the American delegates to the London Economic Conference were chosen without his help, but he was gratified that he himself was named as the head of the group.

The old method of appointing deserving party men brought in many misfits, but occasionally a good man would get in, stay, and make a distinguished career. One such person was the illustrious A. A. Adee, who went into the Department for the first time as Secretary of Legation in 1870. He made his way upward and finally became an Assistant Secretary. In 1920 he celebrated his fiftieth anniversary in government service, at which time Secretary Colby commended him for his learning and his devotion to duty. Four years later, at the age of eighty-four, he died while still in the Department. He had worked under twenty-two secretaries of state. His qualifications for his work have been well described by Graham Stuart—"Adee was a veritable encyclopedia of information, a master of protocol, and a remarkable linguist, but his great forte was finesse in diplomatic phraseology." When Secretary of State Hughes was once stumped as to how he should draft an important note, he called in Adee and assigned him the task. Hughes was so elated with the Adee draft that, after reading it once, he remarked, "I shall now give myself the pleasure of a second reading." When Adee died, Hughes declared, "The government has never had a more faithful and competent servant." Although William Hunter, Jr., Charles Cooke, and Sidney Y. Smith rivaled Adee in ability and length of tenure, too few men of this kind found a career in foreign affairs during the many long years when appointments to the Department, like those to the diplomatic service, were dictated by politics. The contributions of those who did, together with the mistakes of many who did not, pointed up the desirability of getting and keeping ability in governmental positions.

One of the most productive reforms ever instituted in our government was that of the foreign service, begun by President Cleveland in 1895. By an executive order, consular officials receiving salaries from $1,000 to $2,500 were to be appointed either by examination or by selection from the Department of State. This introduction of the merit system into the service was not, however, a success; candidates for the examination were carefully chosen on political grounds in advance, and they were passed with the same partiality. The old spoils system would not succumb that easily. Ably assisted by Secretary of State Root, President Roosevelt continued the assault on spoils with orders in 1906 applying the merit system to the lower ranks of both the consular and diplomatic services. In 1909 President Taft placed all diplomatic officers below the rank of minister on a civil service status. Reform was carried further by an Act of Congress in 1915.

On January 21, 1920, Secretary of State Lansing wrote a public letter to the Honorable Stephen Porter in which he asserted that the foreign service was "in need of complete repair and reorganization." After reading the letter, Congressman John J. Rogers interested himself in the problem and a few years later introduced a bill in Congress proposing many changes, most important of which was the amalgamation of the consular and diplomatic branches into one "foreign service." This "Rogers Act," enacted in 1924, carried several steps further the career idea begun by earlier orders and statutes. A second overhauling of the service was effected by law in 1946, all in the interest of securing and holding ability in American foreign relations. Then in 1955 came a statute of the utmost importance to the Department, by which the foreign service and State Department personnel were merged into a unit.

As a result of these and other statutes and orders, experienced diplomats have become available to our government, both for assignment abroad as ambassadors and for high posts in Washington. Even by the time that Charles Evans Hughes became Secretary of State there were a number of such people around; when President Harding began handing out appointments to pay political debts, the Secretary was able to intervene and bring about the nomination of several career men to key posts. President Franklin Roosevelt named career and noncareer men on about an equal basis to embassies and legations abroad, and his top personnel in Washington was sprinkled with career officials.

We have at the present time, then, a conspicuous element of expertness in the management of our foreign relations; the politician-amateur no longer enjoys anything like the monopoly that was his fifty years ago. Currently, about sixty percent of our ambassadors and ministers are career men. And with the foreign service and Department of State personnel now amalgamated, men are brought from the former into the latter group more easily than was possible before 1955.

At the end of Secretary Dulles' term, seven of the Department's top sixteen officials in Washington were from the career. The Under Secretary, Christian Herter, was the only one who had come to the Department directly from politics. Seven others were widely experienced in foreign affairs as a result of special appointments in the field and in other positions at Foggy Bottom. The Assistant Secretary for Congressional Relations was the only one of the group, aside from Herter, who had not come to his position from a wide experience in foreign affairs; his earlier work as assistant to a senator was, however, a useful background for his duties. The upper echelons of the Department under Secretary Rusk have been manned in much the same way by career officials and men with experience in foreign affairs.

Pleasant personal relations with their subordinate staffs is to secretaries of state, as to others in managerial positions, an asset. Most of them appear to have a good record in this respect, although the details of intimate personal relationships rarely reach the public. Secretary Kellogg had, with his staff, a reputation for irritability. While Secretary Hull had little difficulty with most of his staff, he found himself seriously at odds with two individuals. The Secretary had not been happy with the appointment of Raymond Moley as an Assistant Secretary in the first place, and, when Moley's tactics misfired at the London Economic Conference in 1933, he became infuriated. Having been let down both by the President and by Hull, Moley decided to resign as soon as he could without embarrassment.

Secretary Hull did not get along at all well with his Under Secretary, Sumner Welles, and eventually they came to a parting of the ways. Hull had been irked by Welles's visit to Europe in 1940 without his own opinion being consulted until after the decision had been made. He accused the Under Secretary of disregarding instructions at the Rio de Janeiro Conference, although Welles could give a reasonable justification for his actions. Hull resented the close official relations between Welles and President Roosevelt, despite his realization that the two men were old family friends with the same social background. In his *Memoirs,* the Secretary explained that he had given his Under Secretary, Counselor, and Assistant Secretaries an authorization to deal directly with the President "on specified matters and with my knowledge"; this he felt would not only relieve him of "innumerable burdens" but also give his subordinates prestige and a stronger interest in their work. Sumner Welles, so Hull contended, had abused this privilege "by going to the President on occasion without my knowledge and even attempting to secure a decision, again without my knowledge." Secretary Hull talked with President Roosevelt about the situation. The result was that the President, before leaving for a meeting at Quebec in August, 1943, called Welles in and requested his resignation.

Joseph Grew pictured the relationships between the staff and Secretary Hughes as unusually pleasant. As Under Secretary of State, he was in close touch with the Secretary, and he related a number of incidents showing that combination of official sagacity, personal magnetism, and human understanding for which Hughes was known. On one occasion Butler Wright, an Assistant Secretary, went to the Secretary and told him that a letter had been received from a girls' school in New York explaining that the girls were coming to Washington and wanted to pay their respects to him. Grew relates, "I well remember the Secretary's amazed and stentorian reaction. He shouted at poor Butler, 'Girls' school! Why on earth should I waste my time receiving a girls' school? No, Mr. Wright, I will receive no girls' school.'" The subject was dropped, but the following week the girls appeared. Mr. Wright again went to the Secretary's office and announced, "Mr. Secretary, the girls are waiting outside in the hall." Hughes looked up and said, "Girls, what girls are you referring to, Mr. Wright?" Wright's explanation was followed by "Take them away!" With some trepidation, the Assistant Secretary explained that it would be too bad to disappoint the girls and that, in any case, it would take only a few minutes so "why not take the bull by the horns." To this, "Mr. Hughes tore himself from his papers, swiveled his chair around, and broke into one of his really beatific smiles: 'Don't you think you have your metaphors a little mixed, Mr. Wright? Show the ladies in.'"

· VI ·

The Congressional Front

In his *Memoirs,* ex-Secretary of State Hull wrote, "No President or Secretary of State who has ever sought to play a positive role in foreign affairs has emerged unscarred by battles with Congress." To give life to their policies, a president and secretary of state must be able to obtain a two-thirds vote in the Senate for their treaties or emerge with scars, perhaps as deep as those sustained by President Wilson over the Treaty of Versailles in 1919-1920. They must get Senate approval for their diplomatic appointments. From Congress as a whole they must be able to procure money, whether for the purchase of the Virgin Islands, for the foreign aid program, or for the maintenance of the Department of State and the foreign service. From Congress, too, must come authorization by statute for special projects: technical assistance to underdeveloped peoples; reciprocal trade agreements; or the reorganization of the foreign service. The president and secretary will welcome resolutions from Congress supporting their policy efforts and must be ready to resist those which criticize or call upon them to do what they prefer not to do. In whatever direction they move, or even if they stand still, they must constantly be alert to the opinions of Congressmen, especially the leaders and those who are members of important committees—the Senate Committee on Foreign Relations and the House Committee on Foreign Affairs, in particular.

Even while he was still serving as Secretary of Foreign Affairs under the Articles of Confederation, John Jay had controversies with the Congress. He tried to insist that communications to the Government be addressed to him rather than to the Congress, and he wrote a letter to this effect to the President of the Congress, saying, "I have some reason, Sir, to apprehend that I have come into the office of Secretary of Foreign Affairs with ideas of its Duties and Rights somewhat different from those which seemed to be entertained by the Congress." In the end he won his point, and he won others, too; as the French Chargé d'Affaires reported to his Government, "Congress seems to me to be guided only by his directions."

Secretaries of state or the presidents over them have found themselves in great embarrassment when one or both houses of Congress have refused to go along on an important project. The Senate rejection of the League of Nations in 1919-1920 was much more a blow to President Wilson, its sponsor, than to Secretary Lansing. While Hughes was Secretary of State, the Congress could not be dissuaded from including in the immigration statute of 1924 a clause offensive to Japan. The Secretary argued against it as unnecessary, maintaining that Japanese emigration to this country was satisfactorily regulated by the old Gentlemen's Agreement, which placed the administration of restrictive measures largely on Japan and was therefore acceptable to her. The statute of 1924 would change all this by excluding aliens ineligible to citizenship and making enforcement a task of American officials. The Secretary's protests to the Congress went unheeded, and the law was enacted. Then came the embarrassment. Japan protested vigorously to our Government against the new law as discriminatory and insulting. These notes had to be answered, and it was the duty of Secretary Hughes to do so; he was forced to defend abroad a statute which he had opposed at home.

Secretaries of state have had their ups and downs in efforts to get on with Congress. The statement by Cordell Hull, "I had important victories in Congress, but I also had important defeats," could have been made by most secretaries, although Hull was more successful than most of his predecessors or successors. Some have been soundly thrashed by the Senate or the Congress as a whole whereas others have suffered only minor slaps. Just exactly how much frustration a secretary or his president may have met is not always ascertainable, for, in addition to the open battles that have been waged, there have been many unpublicized differences. Frequently, too, projects relating to foreign affairs have been tailored in advance to meet anticipated Congressional opposition rather than to fit actual needs as understood by the secretary or president. A request for foreign-aid money, for instance, may reflect a generous estimate of what the President thinks the Congress will be willing to provide, rather than a fair estimate of the amount needed.

Approximately one-half of our secretaries of state, twenty-six of the fifty-three, had been senators or members of the House of Representatives before going to the State Department and therefore had a more or less intimate knowledge of Congressional procedures and of the temper and whims of Capitol Hill. As a result of their experiences, they had acquired personal friends and acquaintances in Congress through whom they were able to work. The first seven Secretaries—from Jay to John Quincy Adams—lacked this advantage, for the Congress was, like the rest of the government, new, and experience in it was limited to a few men. The early secretaries had been members of state legislatures or of the Continental Congress and thus no doubt learned something about the nature of legislative bodies. Furthermore, they had made personal contacts with men who came to be members of the Congress.

From John Quincy Adams to John W. Foster—from 1817 until 1892—all the secretaries but four had sat in one or the other of the two houses of Congress before becoming the head of the State Department. Since 1892 the trend has been otherwise—only seven of twenty-three secretaries have had experience in Congress. Both Dulles and Herter are among the seven. John Foster Dulles was appointed in 1949 to fill out the term of a Senator from New York, but his tenure was only a matter of months. Christian Herter, before becoming Secretary, was for several terms a member of the House of Representatives from Massachusetts. Longest in point of Congressional experience were the following Secretaries: Sherman, 30 years; Hull, 24 years; Byrnes, 24 years; Buchanan, 21 years; Blaine, 18 years; Calhoun, 17 years; Clay, 13 years; Forsyth, 13 years; Webster, 12 years; Seward, 12 years; and McLane, 12 years. Although their experiences may have been helpful to them, certainly one cannot fairly say that all eleven of these men were great Secretaries or that all had the Congress at their beck and call at all times; most of them knew what it was to fight and lose. Among Secretaries who had not previously held seats in Congress were also some good ones and some who, like Elihu Root and George Marshall, had an enviable record of successes in their relationships with Capitol Hill. The two Secretaries who had been Speakers in the House of Representatives—Clay and Blaine—and who should therefore have possessed a special background in Congressional methods left creditable records but no more so than many secretaries who did not have this particular advantage. Neither could rate above the average in his handling of Congress. Apparently getting on with Congress is not exclusively the result of experience in Congress. Temperament and political ability are also important.

Political ability, whether the result of native endowment or experience, is in any case essential if a secretary is to muster support in the Congress and thwart attacks by the opposition. Some years ago, an assistant secretary for Congressional relations was designated in the Department, and, although it has been a most helpful adjunct, nothing and no one can take the place of the secretary himself when it comes to treaties, statutes, and resolutions of the highest importance.

Sharp complaints have been registered by some secretaries at the treatment given them on Capitol Hill. Voicing her husband's opinion, Mrs. James G. Blaine wrote in a letter to her daughter Margaret in 1881, "Congress is in session, so we are daily expecting your father's head to roll in a basket." Just after resigning from office in 1889, Secretary Bayard explained to his friend, Carl Schurz, his relief at being beyond the reach of the Senate at last:

> It is difficult to let any one who was not a daily witness comprehend the temper and method in which the Republican managers of the Senate have dealt with public business wherever the State Department has been concerned. I have closed four years of service without one word of amity, of ordinary courtesy, much less of cooperation or assistance from any Republican member of the Committee on Foreign Relations. On the contrary my best efforts and most useful work have been systematically defeated and thwarted. . . .

The Senate had indeed been hostile to the Secretary, particularly for his weak stand against Germany's aggressive policy in Samoa. As is often the case in strife of this nature, party politics was an important cause of Bayard's unusually rough treatment; he was a Democrat and the Senate was under Republican control.

No Secretary has writhed more under the lash of the Senate than John Hay. He was often incensed at the way in which his treaties were buffeted and complained in a letter to his friend Nicolay that "the thing which has aged me and broken me up has been the attitude of the minority of the Senate which brings to naught all the work a State Department can do. . . ." A classic statement is his assertion, "A treaty entering the Senate is like a bull going into the arena. No one can say just how or when the final blow will fall—but one thing is certain—it will never leave the arena alive." Henry Adams reflected the opinion of his friend, John Hay, about the Congress when he said, "The Secretary of State exists only to recognize the existence of a world which Congress would rather ignore; of obligations which Congress repudiates whenever it can; of bargains which Congress distrusts and tries to turn to its advantage or to reject." Hay's final contact with the Congress was disappointing on personal grounds, when in 1904 the "gray wolves" of the Senate defeated a resolution which would have allowed him to receive the Grand Cross of the Legion of Honor from the French Government in recognition of his work for peace.

Although Hay was the most impatient and outspoken of all the secretaries, he was not so badly treated by the Senate as his tirades would suggest. Fifteen of Hay's treaties went through the Senate with little opposition. The first draft of the Hay-Pauncefote Treaty conceding canal rights to the United States was defeated, but it was then amended to the advantage of this nation, especially in matters of defense, and approved without difficulty. Hay's other major defeat by the Senate was on his arbitration treaties, which the Senate passed with amendments requiring the consent of that body for the submission of any dispute to arbitration. This action of the Senate did indeed vitiate the treaties to the point where they seemed useless; as President Roosevelt said, it "cut the heart out of the treaties." The President never ratified them, and they were dropped. Hay's impatience with the Senate stemmed more from his abhorrence of politics as practiced in Congress than from an unusually heavy grievance. He was often annoyed by his contacts with the individual politicians of Congress. Writing to Henry White, he included among the "petty worries and cares" of his office the "unrestricted freedom of access which members of Congress and especially Senators insist upon"; he condemned their "venomous greed" in patronage.

Secretary Seward sustained severe blows from the men on Capitol Hill. In a resolution, a group of Senators demanded his resignation for alleged wartime blunders, as explained earlier, but with Lincoln's support he remained in office. He met with hostility in the Senate to his treaty with Russia for the purchase of Alaska, but he finally managed to get it approved with only a few dissenting votes. Although the deal was ridiculed as "Seward's folly" and "Johnson's Polar Bear Garden" at the time, today we look upon it as an act of great foresight, for a Russian Alaska would be intolerable to us. Seward was less fortunate in his moves to annex Hawaii and to purchase the Virgin Islands from Denmark. The House of Representatives thought the price for the latter, $7,500,000, was too high, although in 1917 we had to pay $25,000,000 to get the Islands. He encountered the same Congressional opposition in his plan to obtain Santo Domingo, or at least a part of it. Abuse was heaped upon him for his handling of the problems presented by French intervention in Mexico. Secretary Seward met these and other altercations with Congress with the equanimity of the seasoned warrior that he was.

Recent secretaries, too, have fought in Congress for their policies and for the Department. Secretary Acheson's Department of State was under fire for alleged communist infiltration within its ranks, and critics on Capitol Hill blasted him for the unfavorable turn of events in China. John Foster Dulles fought losing battles on foreign-aid appropriations, invariably emerging with amounts well under what he and the president had asked for. In addition he was the butt of criticism for his handling of Middle Eastern affairs. Yet, both Acheson and Dulles won significant victories in Congress. Secretary Acheson, for instance, successfully piloted the North Atlantic Treaty through the Senate in 1949, and he obtained approval for the Treaty of Peace with Japan in 1951. Among the accomplishments of Secretary Dulles on Capitol Hill were the Senate approval of his Southeast Asia Treaty of alliance in 1954 and the Congressional adoption of a resolution three years later embodying the "Eisenhower Doctrine" for the Middle East.

Overplaying the warfare that has gone on between secretaries of state and Congress would be an easy mistake to make, both because it has been persistent, although intermittent, and because, like all conflict situations, it has been dramatic, even at times spectacular. Its appeal to public interest is enormous. Actually, the Congress and the secretary or president do not spend all their time in conflict with one another. They cooperate more than they clash. On occasions, they are guided by the national interest even to the point where they seek measures of cooperation and willingly forego a quick party advantage. When in October, 1962, the Congress adopted a resolution authorizing the President to call up 150,000 reservists, if necessary, to strengthen him in the pending crises (Berlin and Cuba), it became clear that the executive and legislative branches were working harmoniously. Naturally, some Congresses have been more cooperative than others, and certain secretaries have had a special facility for friendly relations with Capitol Hill. All are at their best during crises.

Secretary of State Hull has been highly regarded for his ability to get along with Congress. No doubt his high standing on Capitol Hill was one reason why President Roosevelt appointed him in the first place and then kept him on as long as possible. He had an admiration for both houses of Congress. He believed that the House of Representatives was "the ablest group of its size to be found in any parliamentary body" and that "the Senate is the greatest deliberative body in the world." He thought highly of Sam Rayburn, Speaker of the House during his tenure. When he was in the House of Representatives, Hull found satisfaction and pleasure in going over to the Senate chamber and listening to debates. As Secretary of State, despite his aversion to social life, he went to the House and Senate occasionally "to say hello and pay my respects and possibly have lunch with them." This was inspired, so he said, "by my feeling of comradeship for my old friends and by a desire to achieve cooperation and teamwork between Congress and the State Department." All this was a splendid foundation for harmonious relations, but no guarantee against setbacks by Congress.

Among the many successes of Secretary Hull in Congress, his reciprocal trade agreement program rates high. He had long been interested in easing the conditions of international trade and had made this a major policy objective when he entered the office of secretary of state. In 1934, at his urging, Congress enacted for a three-year period the Reciprocal Trade Agreements Act, authorizing the president to conclude agreements with other nations by which concessions in trade would be made on a reciprocal basis. The Act was renewed when necessary throughout Hull's tenure of office, and, with amendments, it has come on down to the present. The Secretary also used his influence successfully in lend-lease legislation and other wartime measures. He worked with Congress admirably in the development of plans for an organization to maintain the peace after the war had ended, and he played a leading role in developing bipartisan support in Congress for the United Nations project.

Among the defeats suffered at the hand of Congress by Secretary Hull was the Senate's veto in 1935 of the protocol for United States membership in the World Court. He found that, as a rule, the Congress tended to lag behind the President and himself in measures for international cooperation and that it was "slower on many occasions than the Executive in seeing the dangers looming to world peace and in taking appropriate steps to meet them." Another defeat which he and the President suffered was in the neutrality statutes adopted by Congress from 1935 on, in which presidential authorization to differentiate between an aggressor and a victim of aggression was not given, as they had urged. Hull believed that differences between the executive and Congress in foreign affairs could often be accounted for by the tendency of the former to look at issues from a national or international point of view, whereas members of Congress are influenced primarily by the attitudes within their respective constituencies.

The most difficult situation for a president and a secretary of state to face in efforts to get and keep support for policies is a Congress, particularly a Senate, dominated by the opposite party. Wilson's clash with the Senate in 1919-1920, more than any other event, has pointed up this fact. The President's mistakes at that time also served to emphasize certain devices which he might well have employed to win over the Senate. Wilson had neglected to take any senator, either from his own Party or from the majority Republican Party, with him to the Paris Peace Conference. He had not cultivated Congressional opinion in a serious way, although during the Conference he did return briefly to the United States and talk with a few senators. He had even neglected Lansing, with the result that his Secretary's testimony for the Treaty of Peace before the Senate Foreign Relations Committee was perfunctory and lifeless.

Among the procedures available to a secretary of state in keeping his Congressional fences mended, the simplest has been to maintain good personal relations with members, especially the key members, and to talk with them freely on problems of policy. This was Hull's main asset in courting the good will of Congress. Not only did he go to Capitol Hill at times to visit and have lunch with old friends, but he also invited Senators to his office, where they were free to ask him questions. He was always willing to confer with any of them, including such men as Senator Borah and Senator Pittman, successive chairmen of the Foreign Relations Committee, with whom he differed radically on policies involving international cooperation. Hull warned his assistants in the Department against engaging in "cussin matches" with the members of Congress. At one time, when his assistants proposed writing and publishing a heated answer to a vicious attack by some Congressmen on the reciprocal trade program, Hull admonished them, "Don't forget, you may need some of those fellows some day."

Secretary Byrnes, too, was adept at personal contacts with the members of the Senate and the House. He showed this in 1946 when a bill to reform the foreign service met with stiff opposition in Congress. At the time, he was out of Washington, but, when he returned, he went to work, talking with influential members of both Houses, explaining provisions of the bill and answering questions and objections. The bill was soon rescued and on its way to enactment; the President signed it, and it became the backbone of our present career system in the foreign service.

The advantages of close personal contacts between a secretary and the members of Congress were clearly evident in the formulation and adoption of the Vandenberg Resolution by the Senate in 1948. The Russian threat to free peoples had just assumed new proportions with the Communist coup in Czechoslovakia. Realizing their danger, several of the nations of western Europe—Great Britain, France, Belgium, the Netherlands, and Luxembourg—concluded the Brussels alliance. What, if anything, would the United States do in this situation? Feeling in Washington was strong that we should abandon our traditional opposition to alliances and line up with others against the new menace. But a treaty of alliance negotiated by the State Department could not be concluded without the Senate, whose attitude was uncertain. The upshot was collaboration between Under Secretary of State Robert Lovett and Senator Vandenberg, Chairman of the Foreign Relations Committee. A Resolution was drafted that came to be known as the Vandenberg Resolution, stating the willingness of this nation to join regional agreements to preserve the peace. Its adoption by the Senate, after hearings in the Foreign Relations Committee, ensured Senate support for an alliance. The Department of State was free to go ahead with the negotiations which eventually resulted in the North Atlantic Treaty of 1949.

A bipartisan approach places on the president and his secretary an obligation, which is only moral, however, to consult freely with the leaders of both parties in Congress on policy problems. Secretary Byrnes has asserted that, with the approval of President Truman, he invited both Democratic Senator Connally and Republican Senator Vandenberg to help him in drafting peace treaties for the ex-satellites of Germany after World War II. This would be normal, bipartisan procedure, but, if minority parties are to be believed, it is frequently neglected.

When a president or secretary of state has found himself under attack in Congress, probably by means of a hostile resolution denouncing or demanding the modification of a policy, an appeal to the people has been a natural recourse. This method of exerting pressure on Congress can be an effective stratagem. Secretary John Quincy Adams successfully appealed to public opinion in 1818 when the Administration was under attack in Congress because of the failure to take General Jackson to task for his invasion of Florida. Clay and Crawford led a movement for the adoption of a resolution assailing the Government. A dispatch from Spain protesting the invasion gave Adams the opportunity he wanted. He wrote an answering note and gave it, with other papers, to the press. The note was one of the most convincing state papers of Adams's diplomatic career, and its effect was soon apparent. It undermined the position of Congress: in the House of Representatives the unfriendly resolution was defeated, and in the Senate it was dropped.

Secretary Olney employed a similar procedure in 1896 when the Cameron Resolution was before Congress to bring about the recognition of the struggling native government in Cuba. Because President Cleveland was away on a fishing trip, Olney assumed responsibility in the situation and called in a reporter from the *Washington Star*. He explained to the reporter reasons why the Resolution should not be passed: It would raise expectations which could not be realized; it would "influence popular passions"; and it could not move the Government, for recognition was a power belonging exclusively to the Executive. Besides trying to reach public thinking, the interview served notice on Congress that the Resolution asking for recognition would be disregarded.

If he is to maintain profitable relationships with Congress, a secretary of state will handle the many requests for information that emanate from Capitol Hill warily and wisely. Questions on minor matters, not affecting pending negotiations, can be answered in the office of the assistant secretary for Congressional relations, but queries of a more vital nature often pose a problem. Secretary Hull said that it was his rule that, when a request for information presented "difficult questions," he would handle it himself and get in personal contact with the questioners. After talking over the matter they were usually able to "reach a mutual understanding." There are, of course, occasions when the secretary cannot in the public interest disclose information which is sought; in 1930, President Hoover and Secretary Stimson rejected a Senate request for documents relating to the negotiation of the London Naval Treaty then before it for approval. Although the law of the Constitution supports the president and secretary in a decision to withhold information, friendly relations with Congress imposes on them an obligation to divulge as much as the public interest will permit.

Of high utility among the tools that may be employed by a secretary of state to build up a spirit of cooperation with Capitol Hill is appearance before the committees of Congress, especially the Senate Committee on Foreign Relations and the House Committee on Foreign Affairs. Prior to Secretary of State Root, the heads of the State Department considered themselves above such a procedure. Other cabinet members would go before Congressional committees and argue for their projects, but, as James Brown Scott has explained, the secretaries of state were "accustomed to look upon themselves as superior to the other members of the Cabinet," and thought that it would be "inconsistent with the dignity of the Secretary of State to appear before the appropriate committees of the Senate or House." This haughty attitude was maintained in defiance of the great power of committees to defeat or pigeonhole treaties and statutes that could mean life or death to foreign policies. Some secretaries would confer with individual members of committees or try to get at them through social engagements, but others remained aloof from such practices.

Despite rebuffs by the Senate, Secretary Hay would not consider going before the Foreign Relations Committee to defend the treaty projects which it was emasculating. Mr. Francis B. Loomis, who served under Hay in the Department of State, noting the Secretary's studied isolation from the politics of Congress, stated that he had very few acquaintances among politicians and that "many of the leaders of Congress were almost unknown to him." He would write letters to committee chairmen, but beyond that he would not soil his hands with the dirt of politics. Loomis did not agree with Hay and on one occasion asked his chief to be allowed himself to go before a committee to discuss the proposed appropriation for the Department; he was refused permission on the ground that it would be "improper and undignified." Hay would bludgeon the Senate with hard words, but he would do little or nothing to enlighten it on policies dear to his heart.

All of this was changed when Elihu Root succeeded John Hay as Secretary of State in 1905. In his former position as Secretary of War, Root had been in the habit of going before committees, and he was aware of the advantages. When the Chairman of the Foreign Relations Committee invited him to appear before it, he accepted with alacrity; he even took measures to encourage invitations. His frequent attendance led Chairman Cullom to remark that "we grew almost to regard him as a regular member." The practice was profitable; Root got his Hague treaties and his arbitration treaties through the Senate without serious difficulty. The Congress was pleased with the cooperative efforts of the Department. No miracle had been wrought, but Root had demonstrated that teamwork between the executive and the Congress is more to be desired than preserving the presumed dignity of the Department of State.

In recent years it is assumed that the secretary and his assistants in the Department of State will go before committees and in every reasonable way keep the members of Congress informed. Secretary Hull appeared, as he said, "scores of times." However, if technical subjects were involved, he sent his experts, "generally accompanied by such key men as an Assistant Secretary or a head of a division." During the Dumbarton Oaks meetings in 1944 to discuss plans for a future United Nations, Hull testified before the Foreign Relations Committee eight times. The impressions made by secretaries on committees has varied. A favorable appearance was one of the strong assets of Secretary Stettinius, as with Hull. Usually secretaries are listened to with interest and respect, but occasionally they are raked over the coals unmercifully; Secretary Dulles several times suffered this fate.

When, on his seventieth birthday, Secretary Dulles appeared before a Congressional committee to testify, he exhibited the sense of humor which his friends knew he had, although that knowledge rarely reached the general public. He began by saying, "This, gentlemen, is my final appearance before a Congressional committee as Secretary of State [at this point he paused while friends and enemies waited] in the sixth decade of my life." At the pause, reporters had been poised, ready to rush to the telephones with news of a resignation. As it turned out, birthday congratulations were extended.

The time and energy which a secretary of state must give to enterprises of collaboration with the Congress can be very great. The work has grown more and more demanding as this nation has been forced deeper into world politics; Congressional support for policy programs has become imperative if American leadership is to be effective in the recurring crises of our time. Secretary Dulles's more than one hundred sessions with Congressional groups during his first two and one-half years of office took him away from other important duties, but they seemed necessary to him.

In *A Citizen Looks at Congress,* ex-Secretary Acheson has given a graphic account of this phase of a secretary's work. He estimated from his records that during his four years, he had had 214 sessions with Congressional groups. Of these, 125 were formal, usually stenographically reported; the others were informal. Many committee meetings took half a day, but the informal sessions were usually shorter. Preparation for the former required as much or more time than the questioning itself, for he was never quite sure of the ground to be covered. With the formal hearings taking one-half a day each and preparation one-half a day, he figured that he had devoted about 125 days to these occasions. This, plus the informal discussions, added up to about one-sixth of his working days while he was in Washington, excluding time he was absent at international conferences.

Ex-Secretary Acheson went on to say that occasionally he had found himself spending practically all of his time on Committee sessions. On May 8, 1951, he began preparing for hearings on the relief from command of General MacArthur, "with work, at the outset, chiefly at night, and continued every day until it filled pretty much the whole day." From June 1 to June 9 he testified daily, except Sunday, and nearly all day. When these sessions were over, he began on June 22 getting ready for sessions of the House Foreign Affairs Committee on the foreign aid bill; the meetings themselves were on June 26, 27, and 28. Summarizing, he pointed out that from May 11 until the end of June, "fully half of the Secretary's time and energy was spent on work with Congressional committees."

Obviously, a secretary may get so deeply involved in these meetings that he is not free to carry on the work of policy-making as he should. He must expect to spend some of his time informing Congress and soliciting its support in policy matters and in the needs of the Department, but the practice has been carried to an excess. For this the Congress must be blamed, for their requests cannot easily be turned down. It seems especially unwise to ask the secretary to sacrifice day after day to such a committee investigation as that on the recall of General MacArthur from Korea, or to any other effort of Congressmen to gain a political advantage.

In the following words, ex-Secretary of State Acheson gave his estimate of his experiences:

> In all these hours and days of meetings and consultations, as in all work, the moments of positive accomplishments, of forward movement, are disappointingly few. Much of the time is spent in what Secretary Stevenson used to call "stopping rat holes." But that too is important work—as one finds out when it is neglected.

· VII ·

Public Opinion

No secretary of state can disregard the public. As Mr. F. H. Russell, formerly of the State Department, has said, "Foreign policy in this country can never get very far ahead of or very far behind public opinion." This fact affects the work of the Secretary of State and his Department in two ways. First, they must keep abreast of public thinking by every means at hand. Second, they will, if they can, influence the people so that support for the policies they believe essential will be forthcoming. The fact that Secretary Hull felt the burden of these duties is clear from the chapter in his *Memoirs* on "Relations with the Public." "Behind Congress," he wrote, "stood the American public, comprising another problem in our foreign relations."

Although systematic efforts by secretaries of state or the Department to maintain close relations with the public were not made until recent years, many of the earlier secretaries showed an awareness of popular thinking and tried to sway it in one way or another. Attention has been given elsewhere to contacts made by John Quincy Adams and by Richard Olney with the press to rally thinking against unfriendly resolutions then before Congress. In handling the *Trent* affair during the Civil War, Secretary Seward saw the need for releasing James Mason and John

Slidell, as Great Britain asked him to do, but in some way he had to placate the people of the North who opposed his doing so. In his note to England, agreeing to the release, he inserted arguments intended for American consumption even more than for the English—arguments which, so he hoped, would justify what he was doing to his fellow Americans. Then he handed the note to the press. At about that time, he wrote a letter to his friend Thurlow Weed, then in London, saying, "I am under the necessity of consulting the temper of parties and people on this side of the water quite as much as the temper of parties and people in England. If I had been as tame as you think would have been wise in my treatment of affairs in that country, I should have had no standing in my own."

Known instances of a close attention by secretaries to public thinking have been numerous enough to justify fully Secretary Hull's statement in 1936 that, "Since the time when Thomas Jefferson insisted upon a decent respect for the opinions of mankind, public opinion has controlled foreign policies in all democracies." When in the election of 1888 Lord Sackville-West, British Minister to the United States, was tricked into writing a political letter favorable to the Democratic Party, Secretary of State Bayard at first ignored Republican demands for the Minister's dismissal. Public furor, however, mounted to the point that, with the approval of President Cleveland and the Cabinet, he finally decided to give notice to the Minister.

The events of 1927-1928 leading up to the famous Pact of Paris against war revolved around another Secretary of State, Frank Kellogg, who encountered a demanding public. On April 6, 1927, French Foreign Minister Briand delivered an address commemorating the entrance of the United States into World War I, in which he suggested that the two democracies mutually renounce war. The proposal received little attention in this country until President Nicholas Murray Butler of Columbia University sent a letter to the *New York Times* urging that serious consideration be given to it. With this nudging, many individuals and organizations began agitating for the project. Senator Borah urged that it be made a multilateral rather than a bilateral agreement. Still the State Department remained indifferent, and Secretary Kellogg said that he was too busy to give the matter his attention. Even after receiving from M. Briand a specific proposal for a bilateral agreement, the Department was apathetic. The rising tide of public opinion finally caught hold of the Secretary; he took up the proposal, insisted upon a multilateral rather than a bilateral pact, and negotiated with persistence until the Pact of Paris, or "Kellogg-Briand Pact," was finally signed on August 27, 1928 by fifteen powers, renouncing war as an instrument of national policy. The pressure of public opinion on the Secretary had been so strong that Professor Shotwell, who had played a part in the movement, gave the credit for it all to the American people.

An aroused public is not, from the point of view of a secretary of state or a president, an unmixed blessing. The people can be wrong; they can make an issue out of trivialities or overlook a pressing danger to the national security. They prove again and again the assertion by Alexis de Tocqueville well over a century ago that, "Foreign policies demand scarcely any of those qualities which are peculiar to a democracy; they require, on the contrary, a perfect use of almost all those in which it is deficient." Walter Lippmann, in *The Public Philosophy*, has pointed to the tendency of a people to lag behind the government in sizing up a situation and settling upon a policy. Although the part of American public opinion in the Pact of Paris was in a sense a triumph, in another sense it was wasted motion, for the Treaty provided no means of preventing war and turned out to be only a pious and hopeless wish. It was a naive approach to the most complex of all human problems—war.

The public which maintains contacts with the Department of State is quite unlike that which interests itself in the work of other departments. The statement is often made that the Department of State has no "constituency." There is within the country no group which it serves in the same sense that the Department of Agriculture serves the farmers, the Department of Labor looks out for the welfare of labor, etc. It does indeed concern itself with problems of vital importance to all Americans, more vital than we always realize, but it has no special constituency of people who give it constant attention for immediate bread-and-butter reasons. This lack is one cause of the Department's difficulty in getting the money it needs from Congress; that is, it has no special interest group to fight for it. The lack also explains why the many pressures exerted on the Department in foreign policy tend to be unrealistic and ill-considered in comparison with those emanating from farm groups in agricultural matters. It feels pressures, but they are often incoherent and uncertain, based on abstractions rather than a sense of close involvement. Public opinion in foreign policy is therefore hard to cope with.

John Hay often felt annoyed and hampered in his work by public opinion in matters relating to foreign affairs. In 1899 he wrote to Ambassador Joseph Choate in London of his concern over the opposition of the German press in the United States to a treaty with Great Britain on canal rights, fearing that the attitude of the Senate would be affected. A little later he told Henry White in a letter that he was distressed about a plank in the Democratic Platform accusing the Government of having an alliance with Britain, because of the effect it would have on our German relations. He and the President were disturbed over the heckling of the British Government by our newspapers for its part in the Boer War; negotiations for canal rights would be jeopardized. The Secretary wrote as follows to John W. Foster on June 23, 1900, about the way in which the people were criticizing England: "There is such a mad-dog hatred of England prevalent among newspapers and politicians that anything we should now do in China to take care of our imperiled interests, would be set down to 'subservience to Great Britain.' "

Perhaps it was these bouts with public opinion that led Secretary Hay to inaugurate the practice of press conferences. He made it a part of his routine to meet frequently with four or five of the correspondents accredited to the Department and go over recent policy developments and problems with them. He gave out certain facts in confidence, emphasizing always that they were not to be made public; this injunction to secrecy was, he found, well respected.

Begun by Secretary Hay, the press conference was continued by his successor, Elihu Root. It was abandoned by Secretary Knox, although he occasionally received individual correspondents at his home. Bryan brought it back into use, and it has since been an established institution, although secretaries have employed it for different purposes and with unequal interest. Arousing public support behind a policy, notifying the people of a new development, justifying a course of action, or even reaching the ears of a foreign people are common objectives sought at one time or another by a secretary. Then, too, from the questions asked, the secretary can get a good idea of what the people are interested in and what they are thinking. Mingled with the serious is often humorous repartee. Secretaries are not obliged to answer any and every question, and, in the interest of the national welfare, they often turn one down. Occasionally tempers flare up, but usually questions and answers move along amicably. The procedure has become a fixture, a vital part of American democracy.

Vague and rather meaningless statements with strong moral overtones aimed at an idealistic populace are often injected into news conferences, either in the secretary's opening remarks or in answer to questions. For instance, at his first meeting with the press early in 1947, Secretary Marshall spoke of the determination of the United States to strengthen and improve the United Nations and of the goal of policy to be one of peace founded upon collective security. That discussion will get away from platitudes is, however, assured by the inquisitive zeal of the newspapermen on the scent of news. At the same conference, Marshall was questioned about the names of men he would take with him to a forthcoming meeting in Moscow and the number of correspondents eligible to go, American trade policy with the Argentine, and the international control of atomic energy.

Secretary Dulles would frequently open a news conference with the remark, "I am available to answer questions." If there were something of special interest in the immediate background, he would be likely to refer to it. On March 22, 1957, he faced the newsmen right after returning from the Southeast Asia Treaty Council and a meeting at Bermuda with the British Prime Minister and Foreign Secretary. Opening the session, he referred to those events and said, "I would be glad to answer questions about those conferences or any other matters that you want to question me about." That there would be specific questions over the wide range of pending problems was certain. Questioners were anxious to uncover, if they could, any traces of a secret agreement at Bermuda, for, were any to turn up, it would be a gold mine of news to an American public always eager to pounce upon anybody engaged in "secret diplomacy." Mr. Dulles insisted despite proddings and insinuations, that no agreements, written or unwritten, had been made at Bermuda. If no agreement had been made on the policy to be followed in the Middle Eastern crisis, a questioner wanted to know, did that mean that nothing had been accomplished and that each Government remained free to follow independent policies. This looked like a trap, but the Secretary wriggled free with the statement, "I would say that the exchanges of views that took place were useful, I think, in making it likely that there would be a common policy. But the contingencies that we had to deal with were so varied and so unpredictable that it seemed to be rather unprofitable to try to reach formal agreement. . . ." The Secretary was never easily cornered and appeared at all times forthright, admitting when necessary his lack of information. At the same news conference a question was raised as to why negotiations with Poland on economic aid had not progressed, to which Dulles answered, "I must confess that I am not as fully versed about that topic as I should be. It is being handled primarily by Mr. Dillon. . . ."

Entering the conference room can be, as Walter Lippmann has said, "the rough equivalent of walking into the lion's den." The secretary has to answer not only questions of fact which will test his memory, but also queries about his opinions and his policies. He must be on his guard against saying too much and endangering vital moves on the checkerboard of diplomacy, as well as against saying the wrong thing. He must be wary, too, lest he offend an ally. At his news conference of March 1, 1962, Secretary Rusk was asked several rather delicate questions that might easily have provoked answers offensive to NATO friends. One had to do with an alleged effort by the State Department to get NATO nations to align their policies toward Cuba with those agreed upon by the Organization of American States at Punta del Este. The Secretary, apparently anxious not to emphasize the project and thus to embarrass both ourselves and the NATO powers if they would not go along with us, admitted that he was trying to get their support but that his main purpose was merely to keep them informed of developments. He explained that it is common practice for the Allies to keep each other posted on policy problems and developments.

In order to keep the public informed and to influence thinking, the secretary or the Department itself frequently gives out statements to the press. These voluminous press releases, like conferences with newspapermen, deal with all conceivable subjects, some in a brief statement of a few sentences and others in extended form. After returning from a conference in Moscow in 1947, for instance, Secretary Marshall gave the press several pages of data on the subjects taken up regarding the German problem and the points of view that had been expressed. On February 24, 1950, Secretary Acheson handed the press a pithy statement about our diplomatic relations with Bulgaria and Hungary, announcing a suspension of diplomatic relations with the former; he noted the denial of human rights within those nations. On April 9, 1953, the Department released statements by Secretary Dulles and Chancellor Adenauer on an exchange of notes between them providing for cultural relations between their two countries.

An innovation brought about by Secretary Philander Knox was the establishment of a Division of Information in the Department. Its duties were quite limited, however, and did not bring it into immediate contact with the public. It was authorized rather to make information available to embassies, legations, and high officials of the Department and to publish the annual *Foreign Relations* volumes of selected diplomatic correspondence. In 1917, soon after the entry of this nation into World War I, the duties of the Division were enlarged to include the preparation of news items for newspapers and the dissemination of information on foreign affairs to Congressmen and the general public. At the same time it was given a new name—the Division of Foreign Intelligence. These beginnings were followed up by more and more activities designed to reach the American people. For some time now there has been an Assistant Secretary of State for Public Affairs in charge, among other things, of relations with the American people. His office publishes and distributes a wide variety of pamphlets, leaflets, and documentary materials. It has put out fact sheets on Turkey, Greece, Iran, and other countries, documents about NATO, disarmament discussions, and proposals for United Nations Charter revision. Information on hundreds of other topics has gone out to interested people and organizations such as libraries, teachers, newspapers, etc. Many Americans subscribe to the *Department of State Bulletin*, which carries both factual data and interpretative discussions of policy. On request, the Assistant Secretary or his Office sends out officials to speak on foreign affairs and provides information, where possible, to columnists, broadcasters, and feature writers.

In addition to informing and influencing public opinion, the Office of Public Affairs undertakes the opposite process—trying to discover what the people are actually thinking and the influence they would like to exercise in a given policy situation. To do this, it analyzes public opinion polls, newspaper editorials, speeches, the statements of radio and television commentators, and the observations of magazine writers. It classifies the thousands of letters and telegrams which come into the Department regularly, suggesting policies or criticizing what the Department has done or failed to do. Assessments of public thinking thus made are placed in the hands of policy-makers. Every day at noon the secretary and his 100 top assistants find on their desks a summary of opinions expressed in the various mass media during the preceding twenty-four hours. In addition, a monthly summary of opinion on current questions is provided them.

The comment is often made that the State Department frequently errs in its effort to discover public thinking on current issues of policy. Indeed, it would be strange if it did not make mistakes, for its methods of identifying opinions is to rely on samples that are available in the form of unofficial polls, editorials, letters, etc. On certain kinds of issues, especially those which do not arouse strong popular emotions, it is probably true that the people are conservative, lagging behind the government, as Mr. Lippmann alleged in a statement cited earlier in this chapter. They move slowly in their thinking, inclined to stand by the present until they have had plenty of time to deliberate on a different course. The charge that the State Department exaggerates the conservatism of the public is, therefore, usually unwarranted. The response in 1937 to President Roosevelt's proposal to quarantine aggressive nations was a case in point; the change in American policy that would be required by a quarantine was more than the people would accept, desirable though it may have been. The hesitation displayed in 1939-1941 by the people toward a bold policy of aid to the victims of German aggression in Europe was another instance of lagging behind and resisting radical shifts in policy. Rumors which have spread from time to time that highly placed officials in the government were favoring the recognition of Communist China have invariably met with widespread criticism.

Where the public is most likely not to be holding back, but rather to be up with or even ahead of the State Department, is on issues that stir popular passions. Undoubtedly the people in 1961-1962 were ahead of the government in their willingness to adopt a radical policy of action against Castro's Cuba; they were angry, their ego had been injured, and they wanted the government to do something about it. By the time President Kennedy announced a "Quarantine" of Cuba on October 22, 1962, there was a feeling of relief in the country that at last the government had acted. In the Berlin affair of the last few years, they have resented being pushed around by Premier Khrushchev and have kept up fully with government policies. Such situations remind us of American indignation at Spain after the sinking of the *Maine* in 1898, which caused a reluctant McKinley administration to go to war; there was no conservatism in this bold course of action.

In considering the relationship between the secretary of state or his Department and the people, the question often comes up as to the extent and nature of the information that should be released to the public, whether in press conferences, press releases, the speeches of high officials, or the public information program. Since World War I, pressure has been on the secretary to give out a maximum, even all there is to know. Wilsonian preachments for open diplomacy, which, however, escaped practice at the Paris Peace Conference in 1919, have had a strong appeal to Americans. We seem to feel that as a democratic people we are entitled to know all and that officials are less likely to betray our interests if they work in glass houses. The assumption is that secrecy anywhere in the processes of diplomacy breeds double-dealing, "Yaltas," and war. If a secret agreement comes to light, the people are incensed. If it becomes known that information has been kept from the public, the secretary is castigated by newspapermen, radio commentators, congressmen, and indignant citizens.

A president or secretary of state looks at the problem of public information from a different point of view. He wants above all to work out with other nations solutions to the problems that constantly press in upon him. He has facts which he cannot disclose without undermining current negotiations or antagonizing other governments. His job, as he sees it, is to promote the nation's interests abroad and, when necessary, to keep things from the public in order to do so, even on rare occasions to the point of making a secret agreement. The people must trust him as their agent if he is to have a fair chance, so he feels. As a cook must be judged by his table, a professional diplomat will argue, so the diplomat must be judged by his accomplishments. As patrons cannot expect to go into the kitchen to offer advice, so the public in a democracy should not ask to go behind the scenes in diplomacy with a multitude of questions and suggestions. Today, every secretary wants to give the people all that can be safely made available. His problem is to know where to draw the line between safe and unsafe information.

Charles Evans Hughes was the first Secretary of State to face the demands of the new, "democratized" diplomacy, when he came into office soon after World War I. In an address to the United States Chamber of Commerce in 1922, he deplored the lack of an enlightened public opinion on world affairs. He expressed a desire to inform the people on the general lines of policy and to give specific information insofar as practicable. But, he said, "it does not follow that in good faith and with practical regard to results, particular steps can immediately be made public." He explained that ". . . governments deal with each other subject to the obligations of honorable intercourse between equals. Each must be free to make tentative suggestions and later to withdraw them. Each has its prestige to consider. . . . The publication of the details of negotiation must rest on the express or implied consent of both parties." In another address at the University of Michigan, he justified restrictions on the information released: "Even the most democratic governments must desire to succeed in their negotiations." He opposed "secrecy for secrecy's sake," argued for full publicity to "general policies," but contended that "particular aims should be appropriately disclosed." This philosophy of democratic diplomacy is one which most of us would find acceptable in theory; its applications, however, in concrete situations will arouse differences of opinions. Where the public has erred since the days of Secretary Hughes has been in demanding too much and trusting too little in the Government. After all, why not trust the Government, even where we cannot see or know what it does? The president, under whom all negotiations take place, is our own elected official. We can chastise him and his party at the next election if they fail us, and they know it.

Secretary Hull was anxious to give the people all the information possible. He said, "I wanted them to see what was going on so that they could realize the nature of the new forces rising abroad and the vital stake their nation had in the peace of the world." The Fascist powers were threatening, and it was understandable that the Secretary was anxious that the people know the danger ahead and be made ready to support foreign policies designed to cope with the threat. Hull began holding frequent press conferences, and President Roosevelt took over most of the burden of making public addresses. Although the Secretary found it necessary to withhold information relating to certain negotiations, he believed that the press understood and that he "had the support of the great majority of newspapers in all our policies."

Secretary Hull's Department published more than had ever been put out before and more than any other foreign office was giving its people at that time. According to his own figures, in the tenth year of his administration 6,641 pages of documents were given to the public, as contrasted with 2,634 pages in 1934. He declared that his principal problem within the vast American public was the isolationist.

Ancient as it may be, the public address remains, for all politicians, a most effective means of reaching the popular mind. That secretaries of state used it so infrequently before the advent of "democratic" diplomacy is not surprising; then the people meddled less with foreign affairs than now, and a secretary felt freer to pursue the nation's interest without an immediate justification of his action and without soliciting popular support. He has always been watched, it is true, but only since World War I has he been hounded. In Webster's public speeches, while he was Secretary of State, were no significant references to foreign affairs, no suggestion that he craved the backing of the people. He talked about resignations in the Cabinet and his own refusal to resign, but he had nothing to say about his negotiations with England and the resulting Webster-Ashburton Treaty of 1842. Secretary Seward's speeches related primarily to the War and its fortunes and did not explain his effort to keep England from helping the Confederacy or the problem of the French in Mexico.

Today, the secretary of state considers it an important part of his work to deliver public addresses, and rarely indeed does he talk about anything except foreign policy. Even in a commencement address at Harvard in 1947, Secretary Marshall described Europe's economic plight and asserted the desire of this nation to extend help, thus taking the first step toward what came to be known as the "Marshall Plan." A year or so later, talking to the National Farm Institute in Des Moines, he went to some pains to explain and to win favor for his Plan, then in operation. Secretary Acheson spoke to the National Press Club in Washington in 1950 on problems in Asia, attempting to answer a question which he said he had often been asked: "Has the State Department got an Asian policy?" In an address at Minneapolis in 1958 on the occasion of Minnesota's statehood centennial, Secretary Dulles devoted most of his attention to foreign affairs

—the United Nations, the Mutual Security Program, and the Reciprocal Trade Agreements Program.

Like the president himself, secretaries have found radio and television useful vehicles for public contact. More frequently than any of his predecessors, Secretary Dulles went on the air to explain and justify his policies. For instance, after attending the opening sessions of the Geneva Conference and then leaving Under Secretary Bedell Smith in charge, he went before the people on May 7, 1954 to tell them about the issues and the stakes of the meeting. About a year later, on May 17, 1955, the Secretary was interviewed by the President on television and radio about his week in the capitals of Europe trying to find solutions to a group of baffling problems. The President opened by saying, "Foster, it is good to have you here to tell us something of the significant events that took place during your recent visit to Europe. You realize that through the cameras in this room your report will go to the entire nation." From that point on they discussed Germany, France, Vietnam, Austrian independence, and NATO. Secretary Rusk has appeared on television several times, usually for an interview; the impression he has made on his audience has generally been a favorable one.

The present need of a secretary of state for a constructive, cooperative public has placed him in the position that, like the president, he is handicapped unless he is endowed with a personality which appeals to the masses. A warm, friendly, and dynamic bearing provides a strong advantage, not only in television and radio appearances, but also in public addresses and press conferences. People respond to the personality of a leader more than to his logic. The aristocratic manner of Dean Acheson bothered the common man. It has been said of him that "his neatly clipped mustache and his 'ambassadorial dress' would have set him apart as a 'foreigner' in any midwestern city before he uttered a word in his Harvard accent," and that "With the wisdom of a Solomon he would have had a hard time winning the trust of the man on the street." The cold expertness of John Foster Dulles and his seeming preoccupation with high and important thoughts cut him off from any intimacy with the people. Both Acheson and Dulles, however, were devoted public servants, wholly deserving the confidence and support of the public.

Present-day methods of foreign policy-making, variously styled "the new diplomacy," "popular diplomacy," or "democratic diplomacy," have, then, added one more to the long list of qualifications which a perfect secretary of state must possess—he must be able to woo and win the people to his policies. It would be sad, indeed, if this qualification were considered more important by a president in his selection of a secretary than skill and ability in advising, negotiating, and formulating policies. It is far better that a secretary should know what he is doing, as did Acheson and Dulles, than that he should be able to win a popularity contest. The ideal situation would be for the American people to be educated, first, to consider foreign affairs in terms of ideas rather than personalities and, second, to give their government more confidence, more room to maneuver in diplomacy without having to inform and placate them at every turn.

This is a subject which no secretary could, with tact, speak about freely in public. To come out and announce that the people can be and often have been a deadly weight on his back would be indiscreet, to say the least. He can state the futility of acting contrary to public opinion and solicit support for his policies. He and his Department can try to inform and educate the people, but they would be the first to admit the limitations of the process, if they were candid. When he was safely out of office, Hull went so far as to call the public "another problem" in a statement quoted at the beginning of this chapter. To ex-Secretary Acheson, public opinion is merely a "fact of life," and should be looked upon neither as a help nor as a handicap. Perhaps, indeed, it is, like the weather, one of those aspects of life we have not yet learned to control—and, like the weather, it can be both good and bad.

· VIII ·

Traveler

Before the twentieth century, secretaries of state remained at their desk in Washington. When foreign operations were undertaken, the usual course was to work through our ministers abroad or perhaps to send a special mission. To negotiate outstanding problems with Great Britain, President Washington sent to London in 1794, not his Secretary of State, but John Jay as his personal emissary. John Adams sent three men—Pinckney, Marshall, and Gerry—to Paris in 1797, rather than his Secretary, to deal with the pressing problems then disturbing our relations with France. Negotiations for a peace settlement with Great Britain after the War of 1812 were conducted, not by Secretary Monroe, but by a mission of three men headed by John Quincy Adams and sent to Ghent for the purpose.

When secretaries of state themselves engaged in negotiations, they did so in Washington with ministers accredited there or with special agents sent by their governments. To settle outstanding differences with Great Britain in 1842, Webster negotiated in Washington with Lord Ashburton, the head of a special mission. Ashburton brought a large retinue with him and for months, through a typically hot summer, Webster worked with them, punctuating the long sessions with dinners and other social engagements. In the end a famous treaty, popularly called the "Webster-Ashburton Treaty," was signed. Secretary Clayton in 1850 negotiated with Sir Henry Bulwer, British Minister to the United States, another well-known treaty, the "Clayton-Bulwer Treaty" on a canal through Central America; it turned out to be a first-class nuisance to this nation.

Secretaries used to feel that it was their business not to go abroad while in office. Secretary John W. Foster resigned early in 1893 in order to go to Paris and represent the United States in the Bering Sea Arbitration. After the Spanish-American War in 1898, President McKinley wanted Secretary Day to head a delegation to negotiate a peace treaty in Paris, for the good reason that Day had been active working out the preliminary details of a settlement. To make him available the President deemed it necessary to replace him in the Department with a new secretary, and consequently called John Hay to the post. When the First Hague Conference met in 1899, important though it was, Hay stayed in Washington and sent a delegation to represent the United States.

The travels of secretaries of state first took them to Latin American nations on good-will missions, not for purposes of negotiation. That the Latin American countries were first to be honored may be explained not only by our desire to counteract some rather rough policies of intervention in the area, but also by our traditional isolation from Europe. It would hardly be good politics to show too keen an interest in European affairs at a time when we claimed to be aloof from them.

Secretary of State Root broke through tradition in 1906 by going to the Third Pan American Conference at Rio de Janeiro. He attended the opening session, at which time he addressed the Conference, but he did not negotiate. After leaving Brazil, he visited Uruguay, Argentina, Chile, Peru, Panama, Colombia, and Mexico, making addresses along the way. When he had arrived back in this country, President Roosevelt wrote to Senator Lodge: "Root is back from his wonderful trip. We in this country do not realize how wonderful it was and how much good he has done." The following year, when the Second Hague Conference met, Root stayed at home, according to custom, and sent a delegation.

In 1912 Secretary Knox made a "swing around the circle" in selected Latin American countries to find out how his "dollar diplomacy" was progressing and the measure of the opposition to it. He stopped in ten countries, speaking at each: Panama, Costa Rica, Nicaragua, Honduras, Salvador, Guatemala, Venezuela, the Dominican Republic, Cuba, and Haiti. He was the first Secretary to visit the Caribbean nations. By his trip he sought not only to understand the relation of our policies to their problems but also to become personally acquainted with their leaders.

Secretary Bryan took no trip abroad, but he did travel many thousands of miles in this country, making speeches for fees, and for this aberration he was soundly criticized. He wanted to go to Europe early in World War I to try to bring the fighting to an end, but President Wilson preferred to send Colonel House. Bryan was disappointed, but he felt better when he was told that the mission was unofficial. What the distinction between an official and an unofficial mission might be was not clarified, and, in view of the fact that House was empowered to deal directly with Sir Edward Grey, it would seem hazy indeed.

At the end of the fighting in World War I, President Wilson named Secretary of State Lansing to the commission he selected to negotiate a peace settlement in Paris. This was the first time that a secretary had gone to Europe on an official mission, and here he was authorized to negotiate. The Secretary was not happy about it, for President Wilson had decided to go, too, and to act as the head of the peace commission. Lansing thought that Wilson would have been wiser to stay at home and make him the chief of the delegation. As a subordinate member of the Commission under the President, his role turned out to be a distinctly minor one, as he had anticipated.

Lansing's successor, Bainbridge Colby, made an official visit in 1920 to Brazil, Uruguay, and Argentina, but he did not go to Europe.

While Secretary of State, Charles Evans Hughes took two trips abroad. The first, in 1922, was to represent the United States at the centennial celebration of Brazilian independence; the second, in 1924, was with Mrs. Hughes to attend a meeting in London of the American Bar Association, of which he was the President. There was no negotiating on either trip, and on the second he did not go in his capacity as Secretary of State. Isolation from Europe was again the key to American policy, and the Secretary's visits reflected that fact.

Secretary Kellogg went to Paris in 1928 for the signature of the Pact of Paris, which had already been negotiated in a series of bilateral exchanges. On the way home, he stopped in Ireland to return a visit earlier made by President Cosgrave to the United States; his failure to stop in England puzzled the British press. The Secretary also went to Canada with Vice-President Dawes and Governor Smith for a ceremonial occasion marking the opening of a new bridge connecting Buffalo and Fort Erie.

Disarmament discussions and negotiations took Secretary Stimson to Europe several times. He headed the American delegation at the London Disarmament Conference (1930), turning over the Department to his Under Secretary, Joseph Cotton. He put in long hours of work in London and saw the completion of a treaty of limitation for certain categories of naval ships. To prepare for the World Disarmament Conference, scheduled for Geneva in 1932 and intended to take up all phases of the problem, Stimson again traveled to Europe in the summer of 1931, stopping for conversations at Rome, Berlin, Paris, and London. He was anxious most of all to reduce any friction among the great powers which might impede negotiations. He did not attend the conference as a delegate, but when it became deadlocked he went to Geneva, ill as he was at the time, and tried to straighten it out. His effort failed, for by this time Hitler's rise to power had fatally undermined the work of the Conference.

During his twelve years in office, Secretary of State Hull made a number of trips, although in comparison with his successors he now appears to us to have traveled little. He attended several meetings of the American States, such as the Pan American Conference at Montevideo in 1933, the special Conference at Buenos Aires in 1936, and the Havana Conference of Foreign Ministers in 1940; he sent Under Secretary Sumner Welles to a meeting of Foreign Ministers in 1939. He attended the London Economic Conference in 1933 but did not go to the London Disarmament Conference in 1935. He went to the First Quebec Conference in 1943 but was not present at the Second Quebec Conference the following year. The Secretary's most publicized trip abroad was to take part in the Moscow Conference in October, 1943, dealing with problems of the War and of postwar planning. Although he was seventy-two years of age at this time and in uncertain health, he was convinced that he should undertake this mission and decided to do so without consulting his wife, whose attitude, he no doubt knew, would have been adverse. Because of Mr. Hull's age, President Roosevelt wanted the meeting of Foreign Ministers held in London, but Stalin rejected this suggestion. Sir Winston Churchill recorded in his work on *The Second World War*, that "Hull would not be deterred. It was a gallant enterprise for this veteran in his frail health to undertake this, his first journey by air." Indeed Hull felt miffed that the President did not take him to the international meetings dealing with the War and the peace to come, held at Casablanca, Cairo, and Teheran.

Since 1945, our secretaries of state have been peripatetic. Secretary Stettinius was abroad more than half the time, leaving Under Secretary Grew in charge. Three days after being sworn in, Secretary Byrnes left Washington for Potsdam, and during the next eighteen months he was in Berlin, London, Moscow, and Paris more than in this country, with the Department in the able hands of

Under Secretary Acheson. Much of Byrnes' time abroad was spent in meetings of the Foreign Ministers, trying to work out the terms of peace treaties with the defeated nations.

Dr. Henry Wriston, in a stimulating article on "The Secretary of State Abroad" (*Foreign Affairs*, July, 1956), has listed some interesting figures on the absence of our recent secretaries on trips abroad. They have been away from their desks in Washington as follows: Hull, 22 percent of the time; Stettinius, 67 percent; Byrnes, 62 percent; Marshall, 47 percent; and Acheson, 25 percent. Secretary Acheson apparently was more aware of the problems created by the secretaries' absence abroad, perhaps because he had served as Under Secretary and experienced the difficulty of doing the work of his own office and that of the Secretary simultaneously. He revived the idea of ambassadors at large, employing both Philip Jessup and John Foster Dulles in that capacity for special missions, thus enabling him to remain at his desk.

Secretary Dulles' travels caught the eye of the public more than those of any of his predecessors. During his first three and one-half years in office, his trips added together amounted in miles to a distance eleven times around the world at the equator. His journeys took him to thirty-nine diplomatic posts of the United States, many of which had never been visited by a secretary. By the time of his retirement, he had traveled 560,000 miles by plane. He had been present at various NATO and SEATO meetings and had stopped in the capitals of NATO countries often on official business. He had attended special conferences of many kinds, such as the Conference of Foreign Ministers at Geneva, after the Summit meeting in 1955. He had landed in country after country on good-will trips, to the point that a nation would feel neglected if by chance it were not included in his itinerary. Despite his continual perambulations and the public interest in them, the fact remains that Secretary Dulles after his first three and one-half years in office had, according to Mr. Wriston, been away from Washington a smaller percentage of his time than most of his recent predecessors—only 36 percent. Near the end of his life, on the eve of his last trip, he told a friend that physical pain would not keep him home: "If it isn't cancer, then I feel the trip is too important to be put off. If it is cancer, then any additional discomfort doesn't fundamentally matter anyway."

When Mr. Christian Herter came into office in April of 1959, the stage was set for him to carry on for the United States at meetings abroad. In a few days' time he was on his way to Geneva for a meeting with the foreign ministers of Great Britain, France, and the Soviet Union to deal with the Berlin problem and related issues. This Conference remained in session, with only a three weeks' interlude, until August 6, and then disbanded with no observable results except a possibility that the delegates might get together another time. Four days later, on August 10, Secretary Herter left Washington for a meeting with the foreign ministers of the Latin American states. Jaunts of this kind continued throughout Mr. Herter's tenure.

The American secretary of state, to be sure, is not the only foreign minister who takes business trips. Foreign Secretaries Anthony Eden, Selwyn Lloyd, and Lord Home of the United Kingdom have kept pace with their American counterparts. Soviet Russia's recent Foreign Ministers—Molotov and Gromyko—have traveled about from place to place in much the same way. A newspaper item of March 13, 1956, titled "Diplomats All Going-a-Visiting," noted that on that particular day Dulles was in Indonesia, Lloyd had just left for a tour of the Middle East, and French Foreign Minister Pineau was in India as Nehru's guest. This itinerant style of diplomacy has not been limited to foreign secretaries, as the extensive travels of Khrushchev, Bulganin, and Koslov for Soviet Russia, of Macmillan for Great Britain, and of Nixon for the United States amply demonstrate. In the fall of 1959 President Eisenhower joined this trend by two flights across the Atlantic, one to western Europe and a second to India, stopping in ten other countries en route. President Kennedy, too, has been abroad on several trips.

The peripatetic secretary of state is one of the products of the air age. He can leave for a conference in Paris, fly back, deposit his laundry, and pack up for a meeting in Rio de Janeiro within the same week. If John Quincy Adams had made even one trip to Europe while he was Secretary of State, he would have consumed several weeks, and, furthermore, he would not have had a telephone at hand to keep him in touch with State Department activities in Washington. Deep involvement by the United States is, of course, another reason for traveling secretaries; we have allies to consult and neutrals to influence in this cold war. While we still pursued a policy of isolation, the secretary could isolate himself at his desk in Washington, but, involved as we are today, there are countless errands abroad that appear to require the secretary's attention.

To the secretary, several advantages may seem to accrue from doing these errands abroad himself instead of entrusting them to ambassadors or special envoys. The secretary's authority is necessarily broader than that of any subordinate so that he can negotiate without the need for extensive instructions. Furthermore, he may feel that he can negotiate with a picture of the world scene in his mind, of what will happen in Asia if he agrees to something in Europe, whereas an ambassador is more limited in his range of views. The modern secretary, too, may feel as Mr. Dulles did, that "talking face to face is the best way yet invented for enabling men to understand each other."

No one can deny that there are missions abroad which the secretary of state should embark upon. But have our recent secretaries not overplayed the idea? Although their traveling is usually their own decision, it has also been a result of the Russian emphasis on top-level discussions, and, to a degree, it is an answer to widespread demands both at home and abroad for summit, or at least subsummit, meetings. It is spectacular diplomacy, exciting and reassuring in these times of easy pessimism, but, when employed too much, it is also ineffective diplomacy.

The spectacular element in high-level diplomacy emanates from the wide interest it arouses. An official as important as the secretary of state cannot travel to a meeting without everybody knowing about it. Aware that something is going on, the people insist on knowing what it is all about. Our alert press makes it their business to find out. Open diplomacy, so open that every statement can be heard and every move observed, is therefore an inevitable part of spectacular diplomacy. As pointed out earlier, negotiating in glass houses is not the way to get things done, for it prevents the compromises essential to diplomacy. After the Paris Conference of 1946, on treaties of peace with the German satellite countries, which had been attended by Secretary Byrnes for the United States, the South African delegate, General Smuts, asserted that its shortcomings were largely the result of its openness. Former Secretary-General Trygve Lie once said that open diplomacy is "frozen diplomacy." In short, high-level conferences must be open today, and open conferences are frozen conferences.

In a study of the State Department made for Secretary Dulles, Dr. Wriston found a number of serious disadvantages stemming from the frequent absences of the secretary of state from Washington. Important among them is his diminished usefulness to the president as the official adviser on foreign policy. Obviously, the secretary cannot communicate easily with the president when an ocean lies between them. During these extended periods of time, the president rather naturally looks elsewhere for help, and always there are others—perhaps a cabinet member, the vice-president, or a personal friend—willing to advise, however qualified or unqualified. Secretary Hull resented the interference of Secretary of the Treasury Morgenthau with foreign affairs, made even when Hull was not absent. The famous Morgenthau plan for postwar Germany initiated by Roosevelt and Churchill at Quebec, and opposed by Hull, provides tangible evidence of the complications inherent in miscellaneous advising. Hull complained that Secretary Morgenthau "often acted as if he were clothed with authority to project himself into the field of foreign affairs and inaugurate efforts to shape the foreign policy in given instances." Hull also alleged that Henry Wallace, as head of the Board of Economic Warfare, tried to take over the economic functions of the State Department. Washington has many officials whose duties bring them in a limited way into the field of foreign affairs. These men, according to Dr. Wriston, will take over the secretary of state's advisory function or meddle with it enough to confuse policy, if given a chance.

When absent from Washington, the secretary of state is unable to attend the meetings of the National Security Council, which also deals with important questions of foreign policy. To exaggerate the importance of this agency would be difficult, as it relates the security interests of the United States to foreign policy. Without the presence of the secretary of state, the National Security Council is badly crippled.

When the secretary goes abroad on business he takes with him a number of the high officials of the Department and thereby weakens it for its day-to-day work. Seven of the top men of the Department accompanied Secretary Dulles to the Foreign Ministers Conference at Geneva in 1955. During an absence, the under secretary has both his own job to do and that of the secretary, all without the assistance of a number of key men. Dr. Wriston described the situation graphically, "The Acting Secretary is in the position of a substitute quarterback with a third team to direct."

The range of duties of the secretary of state is wide, so wide as to seem beyond the abilities of any one man, even with the help of his Department. Besides advising the president on policy matters, he supervises the Department (chiefly through an under secretary), tries to influence the activities of Congress, keeps the public informed, deals with foreign diplomats, attends necessary ceremonial and social occasions, and negotiates important treaties and agreements. On the checkerboard before him, he must play to win in all parts of the world—Europe, Latin America, Africa, the Middle East, Asia, and the Far East. By traveling abroad for conferences or on good-will missions he singles out for the time being one item among the many for which he is responsible and allows it to monopolize his thought. When his stay abroad on one item is prolonged for weeks, as, for example, in 1959 when Secretary Herter spent over nine weeks at Geneva on the Berlin issue, the secretary necessarily neglects his other duties. Moreover, he loses contact with the progress of our interests and policies in other theaters of action. Absorbed with Berlin, he loses track of what is going on in Laos, Cuba, and other turbulent areas, let alone the dozens of areas that threaten to explode at any moment. Without a continuing contact with developments everywhere, the usefulness of the secretary as an adviser to the president, the most important aspect of his work, decreases. The perspective of the secretary may well become so distorted that his work everywhere will suffer.

Engrossed with the one aspect of his work which takes him abroad, the secretary neglects, among other things, those phases of his relationships with Congress which he cannot properly leave to the Assistant Secretary for Congressional Relations or to other subordinates. Often taking with him some of the high officials in the Department, he also makes them unavailable for contacts with Congress. In his first three years Secretary Dulles met with Congressional committees and subcommittees one hundred and twenty times, besides maintaining informal contacts. It has been pointed out by Dr. Wriston that seventy of his meetings were during his first ten months when he was traveling less, as compared with fifty for the ensuing two years and two months while he was absent more. On several occasions, he was unable to comply with requests of Congressional committees to testify, and no other substitute for him could be found in the Department because the men sought were either with the Secretary or away on other errands.

One of the dangers, and also one of the causes, of so much traveling by a secretary is that it is a practice which tends to spiral. If a secretary goes to Country A he feels under an obligation to go to Country B in order to avoid giving offense. If he plays up the importance of a NATO meeting by his presence, he will risk de-emphasizing a SEATO session if he fails to attend it. When one secretary, Mr. Herter, for instance, dramatizes our interests abroad by frequent attendance at meetings, his successor, Mr. Rusk, may seem, both to Americans and to the peoples of other countries, to be failing in his duty or perhaps withdrawing this nation from world affairs if he travels substantially less. Although Mr. Rusk came into office rather skeptical of the wisdom of absenting himself frequently from his desk in Washington, more and more he gave in to the pressures upon him to go abroad.

If the secretary of state were the only person able to represent American interests abroad, his absences would be excusable, but this is not the case. We have ambassadors everywhere in the world, and able negotiators are available for appointment as special agents or ambassadors at large. One of the complaints of our foreign service men is that they are by-passed too frequently; in the words of one of them, "I feel I am in there pitching with no one catching."

Admittedly, there are occasions when the secretary of state may properly go abroad in the service of the nation, occasions when he can negotiate or consult with the top-level officials of other countries better than anyone else. There are times, too, when his personal attendance at a meeting will emphasize our high interest in a problem or when his good-will trips will play up our friendliness. Frequent and prolonged journeys, however, tend to emphasize everything, and, as a result, nothing really stands out. It is like the orator who, by declaiming every point, ends up by de-emphasizing all.

·IX·

In Politics?

In politics, the secretary of state faces a dilemma. On the one hand, he lives and moves in the atmosphere of politics. He was appointed to office by the president, an acknowledged partisan; he confers in his work with party men, some of them Congressmen, trying to influence them and in turn being influenced by them; he, his friends, and his colleagues will be out of office if his party is beaten at the next election. On the other hand, in his job of policymaking he woos votes from both sides of the aisle in Congress; he seeks national rather than party support for his policies; and he may even claim allegiance to the bipartisan principle in foreign affairs. In the light of these facts, can he involve himself and his office in party politics? Should he make of himself a "political eunuch"?

Secretaries of state have solved this dilemma in different ways, if they have recognized it for what it is or given it any thought at all. Most of the older secretaries assumed, and their contemporaries assumed, that they were like the other cabinet members—not only free to remain politicians but even expected to do so. Only a few among them felt that their work in foreign affairs would be handicapped by political activities. Secretaries of recent decades, however, have been made more keenly aware of the dilemma by the greater urgency of world problems and by the formal commitment of their presidents to bipartisanship of some type or degree.

Several issues present themselves to the secretary. Should he take a position on questions of policy which are essentially domestic and have little or no direct bearing on foreign affairs? Should he campaign for his party in presidential campaigns? Should he, insofar as he has a part in appointments within his department, be influenced by partisan considerations? And should he fight back when his policies are under fire from opposition leaders? Of these issues the second, his relation to presidential elections, has been the most pressing.

Daniel Webster was one of the few earlier secretaries who tried to keep aloof from domestic politics and thus free himself for the work of his office; it was the national bank issue in 1841 that brought up the problem. President Tyler was opposed to a national bank and vetoed a bill passed by Congress for its establishment, contrary to the wishes of his Whig Cabinet. Webster favored the bank, but tried to evade the issue in Tyler's presence, carefully avoiding any act or word which would involve him in the controversy. When four of his colleagues in the Cabinet resigned because of the President's veto, Webster insisted on staying at his post, although strong pressure was placed upon him to leave, and he was under fire from his fellow Whigs for not doing so. In a letter to the *National Intelligencer*, he explained that he, too, wanted the bank but he did not believe the occasion one calling for his resignation. He was convinced that his duty to his country as Secretary of State was greater than the demands of party politics; he had important negotiations with Great Britain to carry on. In his thinking and in his conduct he wanted to free himself from the domestic political scene so that he might do the work of his office. When in 1843 he did offer his resignation, it was because he opposed Tyler's expansionism and could not agree to a policy of "manifest destiny" that would add Texas and parts of Mexico to the nation's territory.

Ostensibly, Secretary of State Cass, unlike Webster, resigned over a question of domestic politics. He criticized President Buchanan's refusal in 1860 to take a strong stand against secession. Actually, his decision to resign was influenced more than anything else by his age and by Buchanan's disinclination to confide in and rely upon him. The President gladly accepted the resignation, after first pointing out that other members of the Cabinet disagreed with Cass's position.

A man of Seward's temperament could hardly be expected to keep aloof from politics of any kind, foreign or domestic. Politics was his life, his *raison d'etre.* He accepted the post of secretary of state with the intention of running things, political and otherwise, in the fashion of a prime minister. Although he never fulfilled this aspiration, he had his hand in domestic affairs of many kinds, including those relating to the War, as earlier explained. Secretary Blaine and the other secretaries who cherished an ambition to carry on as prime ministers also had an unusually strong urge to take part in policy matters of a domestic nature.

Despite their agreement on foreign policy, President Roosevelt and Secretary Hull differed sharply on domestic issues. The Secretary was critical of excessive government spending and of his chief's effort to pack the Supreme Court. He thought the President was moving too fast in domestic reform, and he opposed the philosophy of paternalism in government. Although he told Roosevelt his position in these matters, he made it a practice to keep out of domestic affairs unless they had a close bearing on international affairs. Because he was busy with the work of his office, he was little tempted to borrow trouble elsewhere. Indeed, the question as to whether the modern secretary of state should concern himself with political issues that do not bear directly on foreign affairs is answered for him without any effort on his part by his total absorption with international problems.

In the politics of nominations and elections, secretaries of state have often been in the position of being able to help the party cause in one way or another. To such a situation, they have reacted differently. Neither President Wilson nor Bainbridge Colby had any compunction about a secretary of state making himself useful. In 1920 the President asked Secretary Colby to attend the Democratic National Convention at San Francisco as a delegate from the District of Columbia, and he complied. It would be hard to imagine a place where a person could soil his hands in party politics with less effort than at a party convention. Speculation was rife that Wilson wanted his Secretary to place his name in the running for a third term, but nothing of that nature developed. In fact, Colby did not cut much of a figure at the Convention.

No secretary of state has been more anxious to keep aloof from political campaigns than was John Hay. Although he justified his attitude as a reasonable one, it is likely that his personal distaste for politics was behind his attitude. When, in the presidential campaign of 1904, President Roosevelt asked him to make public addresses in behalf of the Republican cause, he remonstrated, maintaining that a secretary of state ought to abstain from politics, that participation would diminish his influence with the diplomatic corps and with the Senate upon which he was so dependent. According to John Foster, Roosevelt argued that unless Hay made speeches the party might be defeated and the Secretary could not continue in office for another term, an argument which, in view of the Secretary's desire to retire, would seem likely to have the opposite effect from the one sought. In any case, Hay did agree to speak, reluctant though he was.

In 1924 Secretary of State Hughes campaigned actively in behalf of President Coolidge and the Republican Party. He felt it a privilege to do so, and, as the leading member of the Cabinet and a widely respected politician, he was in a position to be influential. At the same time, he would not allow any subordinate official in the Department to take part in campaign politics. Right after the election, Hughes notified the President that he wished to leave office on March 4, 1925, when the current term would come to an end. Whether his intention to retire had anything to do with his willingness to campaign, we do not know.

In 1932 Secretary Stimson was put in a quandary by President Hoover, who faced a tough election campaign and wanted all the help he could get. Stimson was sympathetic toward the domestic policies as well as the foreign policies which had been pursued in the preceding four years and felt eager to do all that his office would allow for Hoover's reëlection. The campaign revolved about domestic issues—the depression in particular—with little partisan concern for foreign policy problems; except for the tariff, nothing needed to be said about the administration's foreign policy.

In his autobiography, written with the assistance of McGeorge Bundy and entitled *On Active Service in Peace and War,* Stimson explained that the question of his campaigning came to a head when President Hoover told him that somebody from New York ought to make a speech attacking Franklin Roosevelt's administration as Governor of that state. The Secretary did not think he should make a speech attacking the Democratic candidate. In his diary he wrote that "to use the great office of Secretary of State to launch a purely personal attack on Roosevelt is quite inconsistent with my dignity and that of my office." Rejecting the President's suggestion, he committed to his diary the following statements:

> I told all this to the President and frankly told him I wouldn't do it. I told him my métier was to make a constructive speech about him and not Roosevelt. . . . It meant that I was turning down the first request he had made of me in regard to the campaign and it made me feel very badly.

Because the pressure for an attack on Roosevelt heightened, Stimson finally agreed to make an address contrasting the two candidates in such a way as to benefit Hoover; however, even this he considered a mistake. Stimson pointed up Hoover's personal qualities: his "keen and ever-ready power of analysis," his "mental energy," and "human sympathies." He argued, too, for the Smoot-Hawley Tariff Act, then under fire.

Secretary Hull spoke twice on foreign policy during the election campaign of 1940 to advance the Democratic cause. In 1944 he made no campaign speeches whatever, for by this time his health was precarious. On October 26, two weeks before the election, he made his principal contribution to the campaign in the form of a statement praising the President's election program. To help the cause further, he agreed to remain on as Secretary until after the election; he became, however, an inactive Secretary. On October 2, his birthday, he quit work, an ill man, never again to take up public duties.

Paradoxically, since World War II national politics have been moving both toward more debate on issues of foreign policy in elections and toward bipartisanship in policy-making. Only rarely in the nineteenth century were foreign policy issues, aside from the tariff, emphasized in elections; "fifty-four forty or fight" in 1844 had conspicuous attention. In 1900 the issue of imperialism was fairly prominent. President Wilson campaigned in 1916 on the slogan "he kept us out of War," but it would be rash to attribute his victory to it. In 1920 the League of Nations was debated, although the simple idea of a change of administration weighed as heavily as anything in the public mind. In contrast with the rare campaigns involving foreign policy issues in the old days of isolationism stand the elections of 1952, 1956, and 1960. In 1952, platforms and candidates dwelt on responsibility for the Korean War, peace in Korea, "containment" versus "liberation," stability in the Middle East, the Yalta Agreement, the Voice of America, and communism in the State Department, plus a group of domestic issues. The campaigners of 1956 gave attention to the Middle East (then in the throes of conflict), democracy's defeat in Indo-China, the weakening of the nation's defense forces, H-bomb testing, the Voice of America, an alleged loss of prestige by this nation in world affairs, and so on. In 1960, debate centered on American policy toward the Matsu and Quemoy Islands off the Chinese coast, Cuba, winning the new states of Africa and Asia to the West, American prestige, and whether or not the United States was losing the cold war.

Before the election campaign of 1956, Secretary Dulles tried to prevent too much partisan debate on foreign policy questions. Appearing before a press conference on November 29, 1955, he began by reading a prepared statement, a part of which was as follows:

> Foreign policy will no doubt be debated during the Presidential campaign. Such debate should be welcomed so long as it is constructive and conducted in such a manner as not to endanger our nation. It needs to be remembered that those hostile to the United States and its ideals are not going to take a vacation so that we here can safely concentrate on a domestic political battle.

These words fell on deaf ears. In 1960, candidate Nixon accused Mr. Kennedy of making partisan capital out of false allegations of American weakness and of a diminished prestige, allegations which would be harmful, so he said, to this nation. The Democratic candidate denied he was harming the nation and insisted that it was his duty to point out what he considered to be the mistakes of the Republican administration in order that they might be corrected.

As foreign policy issues have become more prominent in election debates, the idea of a bipartisan policy has taken hold too. The bipartisan concept originated in the latter part of World War II, when it was directed toward an assured entry for the United States into the United Nations. It had enthusiastic supporters in Cordell Hull, Senator Vandenberg, and Governor Dewey. Since the decisive ratification of the United Nations Charter, bipartisanship has limped along, loudly acclaimed by the leaders of both parties, but in practice accorded only niggardly support. Its principal mechanism has been consultation by the president and secretary of state with the opposition, although to a limited degree diplomatic appointments have crossed party lines. The tradition is now well established that the United States delegation to the General Assembly of the United Nations shall have members from both parties. The Truman administration employed Republican John Foster Dulles on several important diplomatic errands. Appointments of this kind are, however, so unusual that they get special attention when they are made.

What is the bearing of this paradoxical development—foreign policy issues gaining more attention in elections, and at the same time a movement for bipartisanship—on the office of secretary of state? It means, first, that a secretary is under a stronger urge than ever before to make political speeches, especially at election time, to defend himself and his policies against attackers from the opposition. Furthermore, with administration foreign policies under fire, he has a contribution to make toward his party's success at the polls, for no one except the president is as well qualified to talk to the people on the subject. To act like a political eunuch in these circumstances is inconsistent with man's nature.

On the contrary, full-fledged bipartisanship would logically impose a limitation on the political activities of a secretary of state. Could he reasonably ask or expect the leaders of the other party to abandon a party interest in foreign policy unless he himself will do so? Could he claim for his party the successes of his office and at the same time expect Congressmen of the opposition to support his request for a renewal of the reciprocal trade program or to vote for his Departmental budget? For him to seek a nonpartisan approach everywhere except in himself would hardly be realistic.

This dilemma of the modern secretary would be more profound, if the practice of bipartisanship were more genuine. Neither political party has gone into it with any heart. Both the Democrats and the Republicans, as minority parties, have complained that they were neglected in policy-making except "at the crash landing." Both have taken the point of view expressed in 1952 by Candidate

Eisenhower in criticism of the Truman Administration: "its [the Truman Administration] spokesmen claimed the entire credit for all the good results, where there had been bipartisan cooperation. Where there had been bad results, as in Korea, they attempted to shift the blame to the Republicans."

The truth is that a genuine bipartisan policy has no chance of thriving except in serious crises—war or near war. The tradition for party strife is deep in this country and will not easily be uprooted. Perhaps, indeed, it should not be. Democratic government presupposes that the minority party shall stand ready to criticize and oppose the majority, not carelessly or irresponsibly, but honestly and constructively; to abandon the advantages of this practice could be serious. Moreover, the party in power in Washington is responsible for policy and cannot be expected to go more than so far in dividing its constitutional authority with the minority, which does not have to account in the same way to the people.

A continuance of party warfare on the domestic front while respecting an armistice on the foreign front assumes that the two fronts are easily separated whereas, in fact, they often dovetail into each other. Foreign aid involves budgetary and taxation problems; the defense of Korea as a foreign policy brings in its train the same kind of financial issues. Turning the relationship around, domestic policy reflects itself in foreign affairs. Little Rock segregation lowered the standing of the United States abroad, and our legislation and appropriation for education affects our ability to compete with Russia. However separable or inseparable a policy situation may be, its domestic and foreign phases will often be so close that party strife on one front but not on the other is hardly possible, except, again, in an emergency when parties would be obliged to quit fighting both on foreign policy issues and on related domestic issues as well.

In substance, then, the secretary of state's present position is as follows: administration policies for which he has been partly responsible have been under attack, vicious attack by the opposition in recent elections, and he is tempted to defend them; if we had a serious bipartisan foreign policy, his hands would be tied, but the watered-down system of recent years is not enough to do more than moderate his political utterances. In 1952, 1956, and 1960 the burden of foreign policy debates was on the presidential candidates, rather than the secretaries, and that was as it should be.

Mr. Acheson takes the view that a secretary should feel free to take part in elections, but "His speeches should be sober and in support of our foreign policies." Certainly it would be unwise for a secretary to make the fighting speeches that we expect of presidential candidates. To do so would hamper his effort to get Congressional support, especially from the opposition, for his policies and for the Department's needs. It would ruin, too, what there is of constructive help from the opposition in policy-making.

Actually, neither Secretary Acheson in 1952 nor Secretary Dulles in 1956 played much of a part in the election campaigns. Both gave speeches during the campaigns, but their tone and content hardly qualify them as campaign speeches. Given mainly to nonpartisan groups, they tried to justify policy, but without the extreme partisanship characteristic of addresses made by campaigners. In 1952 Acheson spoke to several groups, such as the Convention of the International Association of Machinists at Kansas City (September 11) on "The Pattern of Leadership—A Pattern of Responsibility," and the International Union of Electrical, Radio and Machine Workers at Pittsburgh (October 2) on the growing strength of the free world. Secretary Dulles, on October 2, 1956, gave an address at Williams College on "Peace with Justice," typical of his speeches during the campaign. The most partisan activity of Mr. Dulles in that year was his contribution as the writer of the foreign policy planks of the Republican platform. In 1960 Secretary Herter had no part in the campaign, although he did make a few policy statements, much like those he would have made at any other time.

If the presidents allow their secretaries a voice in appointments, the temptation to hand out offices to party men in the form of rewards for favors done is less strong than it was when Bryan went into office in 1913. To the American receiver general in the Dominican Republic, Bryan wrote and asked, "What positions do you have at your disposal for deserving Democrats?" Even then the communication was denounced, especially by Republicans, when it became known to the public. Today a secretary can ill afford to weaken his Department by ignoring skill in favor of partisanship.

Secretaries feel free to repel attacks on their policies made between elections, again without partisan rancor. On May 5, 1957, the Advisory Council of the Democratic National Committee issued an indictment of our foreign policy, saying that we were "mistrusted and even feared by our friends," that "We rebuffed Britain. We ignored the French. We rebuked the Israelis." It continued at length on this theme and ended by asserting that ". . . leadership we have not had." Secretary Dulles gave it little attention—perhaps he was too busy. But certainly no one could deny a secretary the right to answer this kind of charge if he is so disposed.

·X·

The Fifty-Three

Lord Bryce, one-time British Ambassador to the United States and a shrewd observer of politics and men, said that Secretary of State Philander Knox "gave the impression of having cared little, known little, or thought little of foreign policies until he became a minister, and as being, partly from the lack of diplomatic or historical preparation, partly from a certain impatience of temperament, inclined to be autocratic and rapid in his decisions." When William Marcy took over the Department of State in 1853, he came to his office with no background whatsoever in foreign affairs, and he had never been outside the boundaries of the United States. Approximately one-half of our secretaries, twenty-four of the fifty-three, entered the office without any experience either in diplomatic work abroad or in the Department of State.

At the other extreme are a group of men with rich diplomatic backgrounds. Thomas Jefferson, President Washington's first appointee, had been one of three envoys named in 1784 to negotiate treaties with the European nations and the Barbary states, and he had served with distinction from 1785 to 1789 as Minister to France. James Monroe, President Madison's Secretary from 1811 to 1817, had been a Minister to France and Great Britain for more than six years and had headed a diplomatic mission to Spain in 1804-1805. No secretary could boast a more intensive preparation than John Quincy Adams, who had breathed the atmosphere of diplomacy at the early age of eleven, when he accompanied his father to Paris on a mission for the Continental Congress. At fourteen he was private secretary to Francis Dana, Minister to St. Petersburg, and at sixteen he acted as secretary to his father in the peace negotiations of 1782-1783 with Great Britain. When he was only twenty-seven years old, he was named by President Washington as Minister Resident to the Netherlands, where he represented his country from 1794 to 1797. His diplomatic positions from that time on included Minister to Prussia (1797-1801), Minister to Russia (1809-1814), head of the Commission that negotiated the Treaty of Ghent with Great Britain (1814), and Minister to Great Britain (1815-1817). In addition, he had five years of helpful experience from 1803 to 1808 as a Senator from his native state of Massachusetts. With such a background it is hard to see why, as he told his mother, he doubted his competence for the post of Secretary of State.

Almost as imposing as the career of John Quincy Adams was that of John Hay, Secretary of State from 1898 to 1905 under President McKinley and President Theodore Roosevelt. He had been Secretary of Legation at Paris (1865-1867), Chargé d'Affaires at Vienna (1867-1868), Secretary of Legation at Madrid (1869-1870), Assistant Secretary of State (1879-1881), and Ambassador to Great Britain (1897-1898). With this diplomatic background he combined experience as President Lincoln's private secretary for four years and work as a journalist and writer. Like John Quincy Adams, he entered the office of Secretary of State with misgivings as to his competence, having observed the intricacies of diplomacy from several points of view.

Although less impressive than the diplomatic experiences of John Quincy Adams and John Hay, those of John Foster and his grandson John Foster Dulles were notable. John Foster, who occupied the post of Secretary of State only for a brief period of eight months in 1892-1893, had served as Minister to Mexico for seven years, Minister to Russia for one year, and Minister to Spain for two years. Secretary Dulles had never acted as the head of a diplomatic mission, but he had an impressive record of experience: adviser at the Paris Peace Conference of 1919; member of the Reparations Commission and the Supreme Economic Council in 1919; delegate to the Berlin Debt Conference in 1933, to the United Nations Conference at San Francisco in 1945, and to the General Assembly of the United Nations for four sessions; consultant to the Secretary of State in 1950; and special representative of the President in 1950-1951, with the rank of Ambassador, to negotiate a peace treaty with Japan.

Among the other Secretaries of State, several had been ministers or ambassadors prior to their appointment in Washington: Louis McLane to Great Britain (1829-1831); John Forsyth to Spain (1819-1823); James Buchanan to Russia (1832-1833); Edward Everett to Great Britain (1841-1845); Lewis Cass to France (1836-1842); and Frank Kellogg to Great Britain (1923-1925). Some had been representatives of the United States at international meetings of some kind or had served on important international agencies: John Marshall was a member of the famous "X Y Z" mission of 1797-1798 to adjust differences with France; Henry Clay was one of the Commissioners to negotiate the Treaty of Ghent in 1814; Edward Stettinius, Jr. represented the United States on the Canadian-American Joint Defense Production Committee in 1941-1943; James Byrnes was with President Roosevelt at Yalta; and General George Marshall took part in a number of wartime conferences and was in China from 1945 to 1947 as a special envoy of the President. Conspicuous work in the Department of State as counselor, assistant secretary, or under secretary was performed by William

Day, Robert Bacon, Robert Lansing, Edward Stettinius, Jr., and Dean Acheson. A somewhat different background was acquired by William Evarts, Elihu Root, and Robert Lansing, who represented the United States in international arbitration cases; John Foster's diplomatic background was also strengthened by work of this nature.

Although no mathematical formula could be adduced to show what relationship, if any, exists between the diplomatic background of secretaries of state and their competence in office, it is perhaps more than coincidence that the two most experienced in diplomacy, John Quincy Adams and John Hay, rate well at the top in ability and accomplishment among the fifty-three who have held office. Further complicating the problem is the stubborn fact that we have had other high-ranking secretaries who had no diplomatic experience in their background—men like William Seward and Charles Evans Hughes. A parallel can be drawn here between secretaries of state and ambassadors, for among the latter as the former have been career men of excellent rating, like Henry White and Joseph Grew, and able noncareer appointees, like Myron Herrick and Josephus Daniels. Evidently men without practical work in foreign affairs can do a better-than-average job by virtue of a natural aptitude or experience in other lines of work.

Many secretaries of state have gained from the give-and-take of politics a capacity for the give-and-take of diplomacy and a ready ability to get along with people. Secretaries who have held seats in the United States Senate, or even in the House of Representatives, have had a limited means of acquiring familiarity with problems of foreign relations—and there have been a fair number of men with this advantage, including Henry Clay, Martin Van Buren, Daniel Webster, John Calhoun, Philander Knox, Frank Kellogg, Cordell Hull, James Byrnes, and Christian Herter. One subtle art which every secretary should master is how to get along with the Senate; whatever knowledge of that chamber a new appointee can bring to his task will always be helpful. It was the good fortune of William Seward and a few others to have been members of the Senate Foreign Relations Committee. In a similar way, men who had held other posts in the cabinet, men like Richard Olney and Elihu Root, had the advantage of cabinet discussions of foreign affairs and in addition had learned how to run a department. Friends of William Jennings Bryan tried, although without great success, to justify his appointment as secretary of state on the ground of his extensive travel abroad, which included three trips to Mexico and one around the world.

New appointees to the office of secretary of state have not always been disturbed by a lack of diplomatic experience. William Clayton, who worked under President Taylor, both men novices in foreign affairs, stated with supreme self-confidence in a letter to his friend Crittenden, "I will give you leave to hang me like an acorn, if I do not bring out the glorious old man's administration in its foreign policy without cause for complaint even from his enemies." His "shirt-sleeve" diplomacy could indeed have been worse, but he did leave the Clayton-Bulwer Treaty with Great Britain on a canal by way of Nicaragua or Panama to plague his successors up to and including John Hay. Moreover, he went out of office in quite a different frame of mind, as he revealed in a later letter to Crittenden: "I feel like a man with a mountain taken from his shoulders. . . . I have toiled as never man toiled before, amidst embarrassments and difficulties unequalled."

Cordell Hull did not feel badly handicapped by his lack of diplomatic experience when he assumed office, and he turned out to be an able Secretary of State. Indeed, he felt that his background had provided a number of helpful experiences. He says in his *Memoirs* that as a boy he enjoyed reading about international politics and had been impressed by President Cleveland's argument in the Venezuelan dispute. He explains that his five months of service in Cuba during the Spanish-American War gave him an interest in Latin American affairs that he never lost. He adds, "I owe a debt to the Spanish-American War. It brought me into contact with Latin America, the first of what were to become literally thousands of contacts." In the House of Representatives, he asserts, he gave special attention to the tariff problem and to foreign affairs generally. His position in Congress enabled him to have long talks with both President Wilson and Secretary Bryan. These varied interests and activities inspired him to take a trip to Europe in 1925. With this background he felt able to say, "I was vain enough to believe that I was not a novice in foreign affairs." But elsewhere in his *Memoirs* he admits a handicap: "Neither the President nor I had had any too much experience in the handling of the technical side of foreign affairs. We gathered this experience quickly because of the multitude of the problems that faced us at once."

The majority of secretaries, at least until recently, have had vastly more experience in politics than in diplomacy. Conspicuous in their background has been work in Congress or in other cabinet posts, or campaigning for a winning presidential candidate; most of them might be called professional politicians. All but ten of the fifty-three had occupied state or national offices to which they had been elected, usually in legislative bodies; nine had been state governors. Some of the ten who had not held an elective office had been otherwise engaged in politics; this was even true of John Foster, who had been chairman of the Republican State Committee in Indiana, and of John Foster Dulles, who served as an appointed interim Senator from New York State in 1950, although both were primarily diplomats and only secondarily politicians.

A number of secretaries of state had, prior to their appointment, been high enough in politics to have been candidates for the presidency, although they had been defeated at the polls. This was true of Clay, Cass, Blaine (before his second term at the Department of State), Bryan, and Hughes. The names of others had been up for nomination but were not selected as party candidates: Seward, Bayard, Gresham, Sherman, and Knox. Still others had been prominently mentioned within the general public as possible nominees for the presidency: Webster,

Olney, and Hull. Before he became Secretary of State, Calhoun had served for seven years as the Vice-President of the United States. That so large a number of secretaries had been fairly close to the presidency before their appointments shows that their backgrounds in politics had often been on the highest level. It discloses, too, the lofty esteem in which the office has been held.

Although none of the fifty-three was elected to the presidency before going to the State Department, a number reversed the progression and went to the White House after serving as secretary of state. In the early decades of the Republic this was not an uncommon feat. Five of the first eleven secretaries—Jefferson, Madison, Monroe, John Quincy Adams, and Van Buren—became presidents either upon leaving office or at a later date.

Since Van Buren's time, climbing from the State Department into the presidency has been more difficult; the politician with an ambition to live in the White House has had little reason to look upon the office of secretary of state as way station on the road to the presidency. Only one, James Buchanan, has reached the presidency after leaving the Department, and that was several years later.

The early tradition of promoting secretaries of state to the presidency was one of the reasons why John Quincy Adams so willingly accepted President Monroe's offer in 1817. He had no political following of his own and hoped that a distinguished career as a diplomatist would prove him ready for the White House. That his competitors were aware of his goal and determined to block him was explained in his *Memoirs*: "My office of Secretary of State makes it the interest of all the partisans of the candidates for the next Presidency . . . to decry me as much as possible in the public opinion." One of President Monroe's reasons for appointing Adams was that neither of the other two men under consideration—Clay and Gallatin—would be so available as a future chief executive. Henry Clay was a Southerner, who, although his talents were of the highest quality, would be objectionable to the North. Albert Gallatin was foreign-born, a Swiss-American, and therefore unable to meet the constitutional requirement that the president be a native-born citizen.

Since Blaine was an unsuccessful candidate in 1884 (after his first brief term at the State Department), no ex-secretary has had his name on his party's ticket in a presidential election—more than seventy-five long, bleak years. Instead of a stepping stone to the White House, the office seems now more of a pathway from it. Why have president-makers, once so favorably disposed toward secretaries of state, become so wary of them?

The answer to this question certainly is not that the challenge of the office has been shrinking or that a secretary stands out less conspicuously in the public eye. Even at the peak of isolationism, the State Department was sufficiently plagued by foreign problems to test a secretary's mettle: European threats to the independence of the American Republics; canal rights; hemisphere wars; instability in the Latin American Republics; European imperialism in China; the protection of Americans and their property abroad; revolutionary movements in Europe; the rights and duties of neutrals; and a host of others. During the last half century, as the nation has been faced with crisis upon crisis, the secretary has come to stand out more prominently than ever as the shield of the Republic. Ironically then, as his office has grown in dimensions, it has become less and less a source of presidential material.

More than anything else, changes that have come about in presidential politics and elections account for the barred door to the White House which confronts the modern secretary of state. During the first four decades of national politics, from Washington to Jackson, getting elected to the presidency was quite unlike the nation-wide appeal to the mass mind that we now witness every four years. Everybody assumed in 1788 and 1792 that George Washington would be the President; no campaigns were necessary to elect him. Since 1796, no one has reached the office without an effort, but the broad popular front of partisan warfare with which we are familiar did not even begin to develop until the 1830's, for the reason that voting was restricted to the few. Presidential politics, under these circumstances, were not for the masses; presidents were selected by the few rather than the many.

Jacksonian democracy set in motion forces that changed all this. The right to vote was extended and by the time of the Civil War had become divested of property and religious qualifications and placed on a manhood basis. Nominating conventions as a method of selecting candidates for the presidency came into vogue in the 1830's. Later on, interest groups began to complicate politics—the labor unions, farm organizations, veteran groups, manufacturers, and dozens of others. The upshot of these developments was that a candidate for the presidency had to attract votes on a grand scale.

Almost without exception, the appeal of ex-secretaries of state to the masses has not been impressive. Many had been in politics so long that they had too many enemies to be good candidates. Some had been criticized for their foreign policies. All had been working in a field, diplomacy, toward which Americans have traditionally been suspicious. If, by chance, the career of a secretary had been largely in diplomacy, as in the case of Hay, Dulles, and a few others, his availability as a candidate would be small indeed. Besides, such men had never proved their ability to win votes by being elected to other offices. John Quincy Adams, with all his diplomatic experience, would find it difficult to be nominated today. In his own day, he had certain advantages, in addition to the lack of general popular participation in elections, which helped him, particularly his eminent family background and his political experience in the Senate.

On paper there has been a route other than popular election by which secretaries of state have, since 1886, been able to become presidents although none of the fifty-three has found it open, and since 1947 the chances that it would be available have diminished. Succession to the presidency in case of the death, disability, or resignation of the president and the vice-president is fixed by law of Congress. The first statute (1792) named in order of succession the president *pro tem* of the Senate and the Speaker of the House of Representatives. Dissatisfaction with this arrangement led to the second statute (1886), which placed the secretary of state first in line after the vice-president, to be followed by the secretary of the treasury, the secretary of war, and so on down through the cabinet. This left the secretary of state two steps, or, to use a more fitting metaphor, two heartbeats away from the White House.

At times, the Senate has taken the possibility of succession into account when passing upon a presidential nominee for the office of secretary of state. In 1920, when President Wilson sent the name of Bainbridge Colby to the Senate, Senator Lodge pointed out that, with the President ill and the Vice-President's health below par, the merits of the appointment should be weighed in the light of Colby's qualifications as a chief executive.

When, after the death of President Roosevelt on April 12, 1945, Vice-President Truman became the new Chief Executive, he inherited Edward R. Stettinius, Jr. as his Secretary of State. Although there is no reason to believe that President Truman questioned the skill of Mr. Stettinius, he was concerned about the possibility of the succession going to a man who had never held any elective office. He therefore requested Mr. Stettinius's resignation and appointed in his place Mr. James Byrnes, who had for several terms been elected to Congress, either as Senator or as a member of the House of Representatives. In his *Memoirs*, President Truman explained, "Pending a change in the law, I felt it my duty to choose without too much delay a Secretary of State with proper qualifications to succeed, if necessary, to the Presidency."

About the same time, President Truman sent a special message to the Congress proposing a new law of succession. A statute was enacted in 1947, by whose provisions succession after the vice-president is first to the Speaker of the House, then to the president *pro tem* of the Senate, and thereafter to members of the cabinet beginning with the secretary of state. This makes the secretary of state the fifth man in line, far enough removed so that nothing short of a nuclear bomb on Washington could place the secretary in the White House, and then only if he miraculously escaped the blast while the four before him were annihilated. All in all, then, the office of secretary of state has become something of a blind alley insofar as the presidency is concerned, for neither by political maneuvering nor by the death or incapacity of those closer to the executive chair, does he stand much chance of assuming the nation's highest office.

The occupational backgrounds, other than politics, of American secretaries have been law, law, and more law. All but seven secretaries had studied law early in their respective careers and had been admitted to the bar. Another, James G. Blaine, studied law for two years but did not continue with it. Several of them—John Marshall, John Forsyth, Daniel Webster, John Clayton, Hamilton Fish, William Evarts, Rufus Day, Elihu Root, Philander Knox, Robert Lansing, and Charles Evans Hughes—had attained national prominence in the legal profession; and, during his illustrious career, James Byrnes had been an associate justice of the Supreme Court, and John Foster, Robert Lansing, and John Foster Dulles had, in private practice, specialized in international law.

Prior to 1909, this country had only one secretary of state who had had no legal training; that was Edward Everett, Secretary of State under President Fillmore. A man of great versatility, he began his career by studying theology, after which he became pastor of the Brattle Street Unitarian Church of Boston. Later, he studied in Germany and received a Ph.D. degree; then, in succession, he taught Greek at Harvard, edited the *North American Review,* served as Governor of Massachusetts, held the post of Minister to Great Britain, and headed Harvard University as its President. His background as a Secretary is still unique in that he was, first, the only church pastor, second, the only holder of a Ph.D. degree, and, third, the only university president to attain the office. In addition, he was one of only a few editors or university professors to become secretary of state.

Since 1909 five men without a background in law have been secretaries. Robert Bacon was a business man, a member of the New York firm of J. P. Morgan and Co., just before going to the Department of State as Assistant Secretary in 1905. Business, too, had been the career of Edward Stettinius, Jr.; he had been associated with the General Motors Corporation and the United States Steel Corporation before serving the government in several capacities during World War II. The distinction of being the only professional soldier to become Secretary of State belongs to General George Marshall, although several of the earlier secretaries had been members of the armed forces in wartime. His work establishes the fact that a military man will not necessarily be bellicose in his outlook on world affairs; indeed, the lawyer and politician, Richard Olney, was decidedly more aggressive and daring in the office. Secretary of State Christian Herter began his career as an editor, but in 1929-1930 he was a lecturer on international relations at Harvard. Dean Rusk taught for six years at Mills College.

Why has the legal profession had a near monopoly of the top post in the Department of State? Some justification may seem to reside in the fact that the Department has always had to deal with numerous legal problems arising in foreign affairs and requiring the skill of a lawyer—problems of neutrality in the Napoleonic wars, international claims, boundary disputes, the status of the Clayton-Bulwer Treaty, the Panama Canal tolls, neutrality in World War I, and so on. But there have always been lawyers available, either in the Department of Justice or in the Department of State, to deal with these problems; for many years, the secretary has had his own "legal adviser" with a staff of lawyers on whom he has been able to rely with confidence. The secretary does not need to be his own lawyer.

No doubt the principal explanation of lawyer-secretaries is that the law has traditionally been the surest route into politics, and politics has been the surest road to the top job in the Department of State, as to many other governmental posts. Whether the tradition is a sound one is quite another matter. Government and law are closely tied together, it is true, and there ought to be lawyers in government positions. But today government and education, too, are closely related, as are government and business, government and agriculture, government and labor, and government and social welfare. These relationships are acknowledged by the way in which state and national legislative bodies have come increasingly to include business men, farmers, laboring men, and occasionally a teacher or social worker. They have been recognized, too, in the appointment of such people to administrative positions in the various departments and agencies of the government.

No one would advocate a constitutional amendment forbidding the appointment of lawyers to the post of secretary of state; they stand as good a chance as anybody of being successful, particularly if they possess that breadth of understanding and knowledge which the office requires. The objection raised here is against that tradition which until lately brought lawyer after lawyer into the secretary's office with monotonous regularity, as though nobody else in the nation could possibly qualify.

Another astounding fact in the background of the fifty-three secretaries is that the great majority of them came from the East. Were it not for the Atlantic seaboard, it would seem that this country might have been almost destitute of secretaries. Until 1857, when Lewis Cass went to the Department of State, only one secretary, Henry Clay of Kentucky, had not lived in a seaboard state; perhaps Clay's place of birth, Virginia, was his ticket to office. Cass, who had lived in Ohio and Michigan, had a similar ticket from New Hampshire. To the present time all but eleven of the fifty-three were living at the time of appointment in a seaboard state.

Virginia has had six secretaries, five of them during the

early decades of our history when the presidency, too, was under the "Virginia dynasty"; the sixth Virginian was General George Marshall. Fourteen have come from New York State; seven from Massachusetts; three from Pennsylvania; three from Delaware; two from South Carolina; two from Maine; one from Maryland; one from Georgia; one from New Jersey; one from Connecticut; and one from Washington, D. C. In the Midwest, up to the Mississippi River, there have been three from Ohio, two from Indiana, one from Michigan, one from Kentucky, one from Tennessee, and one from Illinois. From the vast area of states west of the Mississippi only two men—William Jennings Bryan of Nebraska and Frank Kellogg of Minnesota—have caught the eye of presidents searching for a State Department head. Have the Midwestern states fared so badly because they have been isolationist, or have they been isolationist because they fared badly? Why is it that Texas and Oklahoma can produce oil but not secretaries, and Iowa can produce corn and Kansas wheat, but no secretaries? And how could the Atlantic seaboard be so prolific in secretaries while the Pacific seaboard—California, Oregon, and Washington—remains sterile?

The fifty-three men who have filled the office of secretary of state made contributions to the nation's welfare that were quite unequal both in quantity and quality. We have had great secretaries, medium-sized, and small. The names of some will be found in every volume on world history covering the past 175 years whereas others, especially those with short tenures, have little or no recognition in works on American history.

The greatness of a number of men who served as secretaries was achieved in another position, a fact easily misleading in any effort to fix their places in the long march of American history. Jefferson was an able Secretary, but his title to enduring fame rests primarily on his record as a Revolutionary patriot and as President. James Madison, James Monroe, Martin Van Buren, and James Buchanan will all be remembered principally as Presidents. On the contrary, John Quincy Adams's work of eight years as

Secretary of State was more outstanding and more vital to the national interest than his accomplishments as President from 1825 to 1829. Nothing in the career of John Marshall, certainly not his ten months' term at the State Department, can rival his contribution to the nation's welfare as Chief Justice of the Supreme Court for thirty-four years. Henry Clay and John Calhoun have had more attention in the history books for their careers as legislators than for their services as Secretaries of State. Henry Stimson, as Secretary of War in the war years of 1940-1945, outshone Henry Stimson as President Hoover's Secretary of State in 1929-1933, although he acquitted himself well in the latter position. Edward Everett has been known as an orator and educator rather than as head of the State Department in 1852-1853. Indeed, his name is mentioned most frequently for his part in the Gettysburg dedication of 1863 as the speaker who gave the long and learned speech which has been forgotten while Lincoln's brief masterpiece endures.

A secretary's opportunity to press his ability into prominence depends in a measure on the president under whom he works. Strong presidents who run foreign affairs themselves take the credit, and their secretaries have difficulty in building up a reputation of their own. This was a disadvantage suffered by Lansing under Wilson. Hull had a similar handicap under President Roosevelt, but with his longer tenure he was able to stamp his trademark more deeply on the course of American policy. It was one of the advantages of Hughes that he had the actual control of affairs under Harding, and everyone knew that foreign policy was his own.

Identifying greatness among the secretaries of state is least difficult for those who served at critical times when policy problems were most urgent and when success or failure would turn the course of American history in one direction or another. Both for the presidents and secretaries in office, these times were testing periods in which abilities had every chance to develop and assert themselves. President Washington and his first appointee, Thomas

Jefferson, had the difficult job of getting things started and relating the new nation to the war in Europe between France and England. It was Jefferson's duty, as Professor Bailey has pointed out, "to create precedent and to lay the foundations upon which others were to achieve fame." He was the first Secretary to deal with the problem of neutrality, with the recognition of a new government, with such questions of protocol as those raised by Citizen Genet, with knotty issues of treaty interpretation, and with Departmental organization and methods. In the all-important matters of policy, Jefferson was not in a position to achieve renown, partly for the reason that Washington was his own secretary of state and partly because the President often relied on Hamilton for advice.

John Quincy Adams had a better-than-average chance for renown by serving at another crucial point in history, the first time that Latin American affairs boiled up in a serious way. The Latin American countries had just won their freedom from Spain and Portugal, and their future independence was vital to our interests. Inaction or the wrong action could be disastrous, as both Adams and President Monroe readily perceived. Vital territorial problems came up at about the same time—Russian claims in the Alaska area and the East Florida controversy with Spain. In all these perplexing situations, Adams proved his mettle. The record of achievement that he left was such that, more than any other, he has been called the greatest secretary of all. Praising his work at the State Department, Samuel Bemis said, "James Monroe made an ideal President. He had in John Quincy Adams a perfect Secretary of State, the most able and experienced adviser available." Bemis asserted further that "Nothing is more evident to one who reads the record of the State Department than that Secretary of State John Quincy Adams stood head and shoulders above the European diplomats at Washington in learning, in ability, in experience, in professional competence, in character."

That Adams was a great secretary, there can be no

doubt; that he was perfect is, however, much less certain. He had little competence in the social requirements of his office. In his contacts with men he was stiff and blunt both in his speech and in his diplomatic correspondence. But he had three superior qualities in relation to foreign policy. First, he knew what he wanted, for he possessed a high capacity to analyze a complex situation and think his way through it to a conviction and decision. Second, with his extraordinary blend of resourcefulness and obstinacy, he had an uncanny ability to get what he wanted; several times, with the weight of opinion against him, he got his way. Third, and by no means least, what he wanted embodied a realistic view of what was good for the United States. To the critical American public of today Adams's support of General Jackson in Florida would seem unethical and even chauvinistic. His capacity to size up a power situation and employ it to our advantage as well as to the disadvantage of the Spanish Empire, doomed even then by its rottenness to die, would offend many Americans of 1963. But his standards of morality were not lower than those which characterized the era in which he worked.

William H. Seward also served in a time of crisis and won his nation's lasting gratitude for his competence. His was the task of keeping England from recognizing the Confederacy and from extending it any considerable help, and of preventing France from taking Mexico, while the Union was fighting for its life at home. Failure might have brought the United States of America to an untimely end.

The beginning of Seward's career at the Department of State was not at all promising. He can be forgiven for his presumptuous plan to be the chief executive in fact, although not in name, for Lincoln was untried and no one felt confident that the new President from the backwoods would be equal to the national emergency. But Seward's scheme for producing unity in the nation by a foreign war was a foolhardy, "wrap-the-world-in-fire" idea. It was on April 1, 1861, All Fool's Day, that he presented Lincoln with a memorandum with the following recommendations:

> I would demand explanations from Spain and France, categorically at once.
>
> I would seek explanations from Great Britain and Russia, and send agents into Canada, Mexico, and Central America, to rouse a vigorous continental spirit of independence on the continent against European intervention.
>
> And, if satisfactory explanations are not received from Spain and France, would convene Congress and declare war against them.

Untried Lincoln was quick to see the stupidity of this project, and tactfully rejected it.

This awkward start by Seward did not last long. He settled down and proved that, like his President, he had a capacity to grow. He merited the commendation of historian Frederic Bancroft, who said, "Notwithstanding his limitations, Seward stands in the front rank of political leaders, both on account of the talents he displayed, and the service he rendered to his country." From baiting the British, as he had done before taking office, he turned his energies to averting war with them, while at the same time asserting American rights as a belligerent and insisting that the English keep themselves within the law of neutrality. Elsewhere—in his policy toward the French in Mexico, in his purchase of Alaska, and in his designs on the Virgin Islands—he showed that he understood the nation's interests and was quick to pursue them. He became a practical realist instead of the wild-eyed gambler that he seemed in early 1861. He was, as someone has said, a good "supplement to Lincoln."

John Hay faced a major challenge of quite another kind from that with which Seward had to deal. He was the first secretary called upon to pilot the nation's course in its new position as a world power. The Spanish-American War brought us dependencies—Cuba and Puerto Rico in the Caribbean and the Philippines in the Far East—and at about the same time we annexed Hawaii. Furthermore, the War projected us into the world scene as a power that must be reckoned with, for we had disposed of Spanish might with ease. These developments did not budge the American policy of isolation from Europe, but they were behind a new interest in China and the Far East, expressed in Hay's Open Door policy. They spurred our efforts to get rights for an interoceanic canal, and they clamped the Latin American neighborhood even more firmly than before on the defense perimeter of the United States.

John Hay's eminence among the fifty-three secretaries is unquestioned despite his indifference to administrative details, his failure to exert himself as he might have in maintaining harmonious relations with the Senate, and his distaste for stiff social occasions. His fine sensitivities, his tact, sound judgment, and forthrightness won him the confidence of the diplomatic corps and of other men with whom he worked. Although to the people he seemed at first just one more man of wealth in diplomacy, little by little they came to recognize in him a first-class secretary. Much was done during his years of service to advance the interests of the nation in the Far East, in the project for an interoceanic canal, in the settlement of the Alaskan boundary problem, and in the general advancement of friendly relations abroad. Hay's part was always significant, although it is true that President Roosevelt was tremendously active in foreign affairs and inclined to take credit. Hay's moderating influence on Rooseveltian exuberance in diplomacy was by no means the least of his contributions. He sensed the nation's new position in world affairs and reacted to it with skill. Shortly after Hay's death, the Atlanta *Journal* pointedly remarked, "There has been a feeling that most of the successes of the two administrations were due to Hay, and most of the failures to disregard of his advice."

Tyler Dennett, a Hay biographer, asserts that "indolent by nature, John Hay worked hard"; he did what few of us do, ". . . he overcame himself." He abhorred routine but he accepted it. At his death an article appeared in the *Review of Reviews* about Hay under the appropriate caption "An American Gentleman."

The crises of World War I and World War II brought two dynamic presidents into the limelight of foreign affairs, leaving their secretaries of state without a good chance to distinguish themselves. President Wilson, not Bryan or Lansing, was in the headlines in 1914-1919; and President Roosevelt, rather than Hull, directed American policy in the second great war. Secretary Hull was not a nonentity but he was in the background; as a rule he agreed with presidential decisions much more than had Bryan and Lansing. What Hull should be best remembered for is his reciprocal trade program, which brought to American economic policy a new approach that was needed. He was also responsible for United Nations planning during the War and for laying a foundation in Congress for the later support of the Organization; indeed, he was always an asset to the president in the field of Congressional relations. From almost twelve years at the Department of State, Hull emerged creditably but without the high distinction won by some of the other crisis secretaries.

Our post-World War II secretaries and their presidents have faced what may well be the most serious of all of our national crises, as they have coped not only with the efforts of international communism to destroy us, but also with independence movements in colonial areas, the problems of new nations, and Latin-American discontent. The two secretaries who, until now, have borne the brunt of postwar crises have been Dean Acheson and John Foster Dulles. Like Adams, Seward, and Hay, they had to make decisions which, if wrong, would bring them and their country ignominy and, if right, posterity's enduring admiration.

What the history books of the year 2000 will say about Dean Acheson and John Foster Dulles no one can safely predict. Those two men with their respective Presidents were the chief builders of the dam behind which the free world now holds off the flood of communism. A beginning had been made, a good beginning, by the Marshall-Truman administration (in which Acheson deserves some recognition as Under Secretary) in the enunciation of the Truman Doctrine of aid to Greece and Turkey and in the Marshall Plan for Europe. The Acheson-Truman team carried further the policy of containment with NATO, the mutual security program, and the protection of Korea; it took defensible positions on the German problem, disarmament, and technical assistance. Secretary Dulles extended our alliance system and strengthened the mechanism of containment, especially in Asia.

Unfair as it may be, history's estimate of Acheson and Dulles may depend on how well the secretaries and presidents after them keep in repair the dam they built. If the free world ultimately emerges from the cold war, independent and stable, they will be heroes for their work. If it goes under or if a hot war ensues, the remaining Americans, if any, will be in a mood to condemn all who had a part in the diplomacy of our era. At this date, however, we can safely say that both Secretaries, despite the aspersions heaped upon them, displayed impressive ability in office.

In addition to the men who have proved their greatness in the midst of serious national danger, there are others who in more quiet times have exhibited high competence in the office of secretary of state. Their faithfulness and skill were clearly evident, although not applied to world-shaking problems. After all, a man may have been a competent secretary without saving us from destruction or moving us forward from an era of deep uncertainty into serenity.

Daniel Webster has always been looked upon as belonging to this category of secretaries. His four years in office, divided into two stretches of two years each, were not beleagured with challenges. His most notable achievement was the conclusion of the Treaty of Washington settling outstanding issues with Great Britain. In this work he showed himself to be an able negotiator, with a capacity for compromise more necessary to the art of diplomacy than critical Americans always realize. In the *North American Review* for 1849 was a review of *Diplomatic and State Papers of Daniel Webster* as Secretary of State. Although so laudatory of Webster that, written about anyone else it would have seemed in bad taste, about him it was not wildly extravagant. It mentioned "his great powers, experience and patriotic feeling," his "unrivalled English," and his "wise and reflecting spirit, careful for the welfare of his country, and studious from afar of the things that made for its happiness and renown." Like Adams, he was a patriot, and, also like Adams, he paraded his patriotism openly. In the famous "Hulsemann note" to the Austrian Chargé d'Affaires, there was not only a convincing exposition of the de facto policy of recognition but also vigorous reproof and boasting intended to arouse national pride at home and to awaken the governments of Europe to our growing greatness. He wrote, "The power of this republic at the present time is spread over a region one of the richest and most fertile of the globe, and of an extent in comparison with which the possessions of the House of Hapsburg are but a patch on the earth's surface. . . ." Although the note sounded good to American ears, its harshness and its swagger were not justified, and it detracts even today from the high esteem in which we hold its author. Like Adams, Webster, too, was a realist, concerned for the welfare of the nation. In his biography of Webster, the elder Henry Cabot Lodge gave his opinion of the Secretary's place in history: "It may fairly be said that no one, with the exception of John Quincy Adams, has ever shown higher qualities or attained greater success in the administration of the State Department, than Mr. Webster did while in Mr. Tyler's Cabinet."

Several secretaries of this present century have won more than an average amount of admiration although they left no great monument of accomplishment. Root was highly regarded for his agreement with Japan on immigration, his arbitration treaties, his interest in Latin America, and the work of his delegation at the Hague Conference (1907). Hughes, even more than Root, has been cited for high competence. He came to the Department soon after the nation had rejected Wilson's League of Nations and had slunk back into its isolationist shell. It wanted no hero in the State Department. Hughes could add little to the American position in world affairs because nobody wanted any position at all; he could not strengthen American leadership because nobody wanted to lead. He was also handicapped by the new style of open diplomacy that has prevailed since World War I. What there was to be done, Hughes did with distinction, and he found more to do than anyone would have thought possible. In a masterly manner, he arranged and carried through to completion the Washington Disarmament Conference of 1921-1922. His Latin American policy was constructive, impressing upon the people of this hemisphere the fact that "We covet no territory" and that we have ". . . no policy which runs counter to your national aspirations and no purpose save to promote the interests of peace." He sponsored the Central American Conference of 1923 to deal with procedures for maintaining the peace in that area, and, to further the cause of inter-American harmony, he made a trip to Brazil.

Only a few secretaries have been notoriously inadequate. Three—Smith, Cass, and Sherman—came close to a tie for their incompetence; Cass and Sherman had been able men in politics but were too old to be useful when they came to the State Department. What Graham Stuart said of Smith might be applied to all three: ". . . today he is one of the Secretaries of State whose name is practically forgotten."

· XI ·

His Philosophy

Even though he may never have reasoned systematically about the subject, every secretary of state, and indeed everybody who thinks about foreign affairs at all, starts with certain assumptions, principles, and beliefs which collectively constitute his philosophy of international politics. Secretary Hull recognized the bearing of fundamental principles upon his conduct in office when he said of President Roosevelt, "He and I entertained in most respects the same philosophy in international relations." However simplifying it would be, the position cannot be honestly taken that Republican secretaries have consistently espoused one philosophy and Democrats another.

Isolationism was for many years a basic tenet of secretaries of state, as it was of all Americans. It was supported by argument in some instances, but more often it was just assumed. Our first Secretary, Thomas Jefferson, was well aware of the dangers of the European balance-of-power system and wanted to keep clear of it. Later, as President, he laid down the rule of no "entangling alliances," thus affirming President Washington's counsel against "permanent alliances." Isolationist philosophy crept into many state papers for which later secretaries were either partly or wholly responsible. It was, for instance, suggested but not openly advanced in the language of the Monroe Doctrine (1823), and it was embodied in Webster's famous note to Chevalier Hulsemann, Austria's Chargé d'Affaires to the United States, in 1850.

Although Secretary Olney's policies constituted no challenge to isolationism and his state papers (e.g., the "Olney Corollary" note to Ambassador Bayard in 1895) seemed in places to be tinged with isolationist philosophy, after leaving office he wrote an article entitled "The International Isolation of the United States" for the *Atlantic Monthly* which was a definite commitment to internationalism. In it he pointed out the folly of this nation's trying "to seclude itself from the world at large and to live a life as insulated and independent as if it were the only country on the footstool." He argued, "A nation is as much a member of society as an individual," and "The individual who should deliberately undertake to ignore society and social obligations, to mix with his kind only under compulsion, to abstain from all effort to make men wiser or happier, to resist all appeals to charity . . . would be universally condemned." He believed that an "isolation that is nothing but a shirking of the responsibilities of high place and great power is simply ignominious." But he did not think that ceasing to be a "recluse" would necessarily bring us into formal alliances with other nations. This philosophy was heresy in those days.

Since World War I secretaries have moved further and further away from isolationism, faster as a rule than the people. Secretary Hughes was cautious in his policy toward the League of Nations, fearful of the obligations that the United States would have to assume in its collective security system if we were to become a member. In 1923, however, he initiated a long period of cooperation with the League in its nonpolitical activities by sending delegates to a conference at Geneva on communication and transit. He was a strong proponent of American membership in the World Court. Secretary Kellogg, too, was a cautious internationalist, cooperating with the League and advocating membership in the Court. Secretary Stimson's position was quite similar, although he and President Hoover went still further in cooperating with the League, even so far as to have a delegate present at a Council meeting on the Manchurian crisis, a political problem.

Secretary Hull called himself a "moderate" in international relations, veering away from the two extremes of his time. He said, "One is the view of extreme internationalism which rests upon the idea of political commitments. We keep entirely away from that in our thoughts and views and policies, just as we seek, on the other hand, to keep entirely away from the extreme nationalists. . . ." Although he made it clear that he was no disciple of that school of thought which would surrender all or most of the nation's sovereign powers to a world organization, he was nevertheless strongly in favor of international cooperation. He had earlier supported the League of Nations, and, as Secretary of State, he played a leading role in the development of the United Nations. He flayed the isolationists and argued that ". . . the United States had to assume her full responsibility in the world." His internationalism, however, was not the kind that would support balance-of-power politics; he was not, as he explained, ". . . a believer in the idea of balance of power or spheres of influence as a means of keeping the peace." His philosophy emphasized, in addition to the United Nations idea, the economic bases of peace.

Hull's successors in office were internationalists not only in the sense of supporting the United Nations but also in taking a strong part in the affairs of Europe and in power politics. Secretary Stettinius continued Hull's work in the creation of the United Nations, and he had a part in Yalta and other political developments of the period. Byrnes, while backing the United Nations, was active at many international meetings which endeavored to rearrange the affairs of Europe after the War. Marshall supported the "Truman Doctrine" of aid to Greece, Turkey, and any other nation seeking to defend itself against communism; he was the prime mover in the "Marshall Plan" for strengthening the nations of western Europe.

The longest strides into world politics were taken while Dean Acheson and John Foster Dulles were in office, the two of them responsible, together with Presidents Truman and Eisenhower, for American participation and leadership in peacetime alliances, which for more than a century and a half had been anathematized by our political leaders. Under Acheson and Truman, the NATO alliance was constructed; a few years later Dulles and Eisenhower took the initiative in working out SEATO and in giving inspiration and assistance to the Baghdad group. We have, as Acheson phrased it, been "facing up to our responsibilities seriously and honestly, without any sugar-coating, without trying to deceive ourselves." At the present time, a secretary of state with the isolationist philosophy of our nineteenth-century secretaries would seem as strange as a mastodon and of something like the same intelligence.

Legalism has always played a strong part in the philosophies of American secretaries of state. This has been an inevitable result of the fact that secretaries have come, almost without exception until recently, from the legal profession. They have been inclined to emphasize the arbitration of international disputes, and often they have taken a personal hand in cases to which the United States has been a party, as John Foster did in the Bering Sea arbitration (1892-1893). Secretaries Olney, Hay, Root, Bryan, and Kellogg all sponsored bilateral arbitration treaties by which international disputes would be settled by law. It was characteristic of law-minded secretaries that Hughes, Kellogg, and Stimson should be cautious toward the League of Nations but enthusiastic for American membership in the World Court. The manner in which Secretary of State Lansing labored the legal aspects of American neutrality in his notes to Germany in World War I was also rather typical of the approach of a secretary trained in law. The legal background of Secretary Hughes showed up so much in his work that he has been referred to as a "diplomat of legalism."

In the book, *American Diplomacy, 1900-1950,* Mr. George Kennan said, "I see the most serious fault of our past policy formulation to lie in something that I might call the legalistic-moralistic approach to international problems." That attention to the legal aspects of policy will be excessive when it precludes a proper consideration of economic and security interests can scarcely be doubted. The first concern of a policy-maker must be the life of his nation, and for him to devote his major effort to legalistic niceties while enemies plot its extermination could be fatal. Focusing on the law in international relations easily leads to an oversimplification of world affairs. War, for instance, will appear principally as the result of the inadequacies of international law rather than of the many complicated forces and pressures which modern civilization harbors—nationalism, imperialism, conflicting ideologies, economic rivalries, and an endless competition for power. An unswerving determination to adhere to the law, come what may, inclines a policy-maker to ascribe to the officials of other nations a like respect for legal conduct and therefore to be duped by the promises of an opponent who is less conscientious. Our government after World War II relied in vain on commitments made by the Russians at Yalta, and more recently it was deceived by an informal pledge of the Soviet Government to maintain a moratorium on nuclear testing, a pledge abruptly broken in September, 1961.

The other extreme in conduct, disregard of law, can be quite as fatal as total subservience to it. No nation will profit from a reputation for breaking the law; as with an individual, honesty is good policy. It produces confidence in community relationships; it wins friends and perhaps allies; and it imparts stability and force to rules of conduct which at some future time may serve the interests of a nation presently tempted to break them. Unless nations become more disposed to follow law than they now are, it is difficult to see how they can progress from the anarchy of war to a reliable peace. The policy-maker therefore finds himself, at this particular stage of international relations, in the position of having to avoid extremes—that is, he can give neither slavish obedience to the law nor careless indifference to it without risking the present and future welfare of his country and of the world community.

Although American secretaries of state have displayed a greater-than-average attention to law in international affairs, they have not, even the most legally minded among them, been totally oblivious to the nonlegal facts of life. Despite his legalism, Secretary Hughes was quite aware of the national interests. More than ever since World War II secretaries have dealt with the security and power phases of world politics with understanding and skill, although they have also placed more reliance on the word of the Soviet Union than was justified. To what extent this broadened outlook has resulted from the fact that they have less often than formerly been lawyers and have come from stronger backgrounds in diplomacy is conjectural.

Nothing in the philosophies of international relations held by secretaries of state has been more significant than the extent to which they have embodied attitudes referred to as "realism" and "idealism." Any discussion of this subject must begin with an admission that "realism" and "idealism" are slippery concepts; what may seem to one person to be an idealistic course of action will appear to another as realistic. A realist is commonly defined as a person who thinks in terms of things as they are, while the idealist bases his thought processes on what ought to be. Whereas the former accepts the world for what it is and bows to its demands, the latter strives for something better. In foreign policy the two philosophies will look differently upon the national interest; realism will accept it as a complete guide to conduct and will incline toward a selfish interpretation of what it is whereas idealism tends to renounce it as sordid or to identify it with the broader world interest. By taking international politics as he finds them and being skeptical of reform, the realist will not be too circumspect in the policies which he adopts in pursuance of the national interest; legal and ethical irregularities, although not preferred, will be condoned, and the use of power—military and nonmilitary—will be regarded as normal and indeed inevitable. The idealist, intent on a better world, is more insistent on legal and ethical standards in national conduct; he abhors military power and the balance of power and works for their eradication or for a reduction of their role.

Where realism ends and idealism begins can never be a fixed, immutable line. The idealist will say, and he may be right, that there is realism in idealism, that it is in the national interest to promote a good world and to pursue national objectives only by ethical means. Most complicating in the use of such terms is the fact that they are not mutually exclusive; instead of being a confirmed realist or a confirmed idealist, men represent varying combinations of the two, differing from each other only in degree or in emphasis. This has been true of our secretaries of state in their outlook on international relations. All have been in part realistic and in part idealistic. All have used the language of idealism as every public official in this nation must; some have very likely meant exactly what they said, but others were courting the support of ethically minded Americans. Usually from his actions more than from his words, a secretary has been so dominantly one or the other that it seems fair to pin either the label "realist" or that of "idealist" to his philosophy of international affairs.

President Washington's first appointee as Secretary of State, Thomas Jefferson, displayed a striking combination of idealism and realism. Idealism showed up in his sympathy with the cause of the French Revolution. In a letter to a friend, he wrote that, rather than see the Revolution fail, "I would have seen half the earth desolated; were there but an Adam and Eve left in every country, and left free, it would be better than it is now." A democratic world would, in his opinion, be a better one and one in which all could live more securely. Consequently, he stood for the recognition of the Revolutionary regime in France and the acceptance of Citizen Genet as its Minister. Although his idealism committed him to the Revolution, Jefferson's realism rejected the idea of American participation in the Franco-British War, then being waged, because of the harm it would do to this nation; the national interest could be best served by staying clear of Europe's quarrels. He rightly argued, against Alexander Hamilton's pro-British views, that the Franco-American Treaty of Alliance of 1778 was still legally binding upon us, but he hoped that France would not ask for help under its terms —and in fact she did not. With the rest of the Cabinet, therefore, Jefferson approved the substance of the Neutrality Proclamation of 1793, but he insisted that the word "neutrality" not be incorporated into it.

No nineteenth-century secretary could match the realism of John Quincy Adams, although even he was not without an element of idealism in his outlook. Cold and calculating, he bent his energy toward the promotion of the national interest by strengthening its material position and its security. Professor Samuel Bemis, one of his biographers, has aptly said that it was "characteristic of John Quincy Adams that when the circumstances forced him to shift a political position, he was able to rationalize his action." It was like him as a peace Commissioner at Ghent in 1814, before becoming Secretary, to concede to the British a right to the navigation of the Mississippi River, which would be worthless to them, in return for valuable fishing rights to Americans in the North Atlantic. One of his hard-headed moves as Secretary was to defend General Jackson's unauthorized invasion of Spanish East Florida in 1818. His argument at that time was so cogent that it is often called his strongest state paper. To the Spanish protest against the invasion, Adams answered that the act was one of self-defense. Then he took the offensive, with the acquisition of East Florida his objective, pointing out that Spain had not been able to control the Indians in the area. He notified the Spanish Government that it must either place adequate forces there or cede it to the United States. Finally, in 1819, Adams negotiated a treaty with Spain for the purchase of East Florida, to be paid by surrendering the claims of Americans against Spain, valued at $5,000,000, and giving up a tenuous claim to Texas.

In the formulation of the Monroe Doctrine, realism once again marked Adams's statesmanship. Like President Monroe and other leading Americans, he saw the danger to the security of the United States presented by the threat of the Holy Alliance to restore the colonies of Spain. But, with a greater shrewdness than his colleagues exhibited, he sized up the power situation within the Alliance. Great Britain, like the United States, opposed the return of the colonies to the Spanish yoke and suggested to Richard Rush, our Minister in London, that the two governments issue a joint pronouncement against reconquest. The vital issue was, therefore, whether the United States should combine with Britain or stand alone. Both Thomas Jefferson and James Madison, who were consulted by the President, counseled in favor of cooperation. Adams alone argued for a unilateral statement, maintaining that, in cooperation with Britain, we would necessarily play the lesser role because of our relative weakness and that the interests of the British, coinciding with our own, would in any case assure us of her support, were a crisis to arise. The Secretary saw, too, that a joint statement would place the United States and Britain on the same plane insofar as future acquisitions of territory in this hemisphere were concerned, and he realized that in time we might want to add California, Texas, or Cuba to the national domain. In his mind it was clear that to act alone would serve our interests better than "to come in as a cock boat in the wake of the British man-of-war." The wisdom of his counsel was recognized.

Adams saw clearly the importance to the United States of expanding its territorial holdings on this continent. Although the term "manifest destiny" was not coined until years later, he put himself on record as believing in the idea it embodied. He said:

> The whole continent of North America appears to be destined by Divine Providence to be peopled by one nation, speaking one language, professing one general system of religious and political principles, and accustomed to one general tenor of social usages and customs. For the common happiness of them all, I believe it indispensable that they should be associated in one federal union.

This statement shows not only his ambition for the greatness of his country but also his capacity to clothe hard-headed, even selfish ideas, in the phraseology of moralism. In this, he was by no means unique among secretaries of state and presidents.

Secretary Adams had a place in his philosophy of international relations for the reforms of the idealist, but certainly he did not devote much time or effort toward their achievement. He contended, "the more of pure moral principle is carried into the policy and conduct of a government, the wiser and more profound will that policy be." He favored the development of international law, but, significantly, he was most interested in a statement of neutral rights favorable to the United States—the freedom of enemy property on a neutral ship and of neutral property on an enemy ship, and a restriction of contraband.

Probably no secretary of state has been more committed to idealism and ethics in foreign affairs than William Jennings Bryan. His utterances and his actions had little or no relevance to the security interests of the nation or to the realities of the power system in which we were obliged to live. He wanted peace above all else—a worthy aspiration, to be sure—but he sought it without taking cognizance of the tough realities of the international political system facing him. We can believe Mrs. Bryan's statement that "None of his work gave him more pleasure than his peace treaties." The President gave him a free hand with these treaties, although on most matters of foreign policy Wilson dominated. Bryan concluded thirty of these treaties providing for the compulsory investigation of disputes not otherwise handled and a "cooling off period" in which the investigating committee would prepare a report.

Bryan's unrealistic outlook in foreign affairs seems rather strange in view of his considerable ability to understand and face the facts of life in national politics. He played to win in party politics, looking upon it as right and proper. He found the methods of international politics to revolve so much more around power in the form of force than in the form of votes, as in national affairs, that he was more interested in cleaning up than in playing the game. If he deigned to play at all, he could think only of the moral phases of action, what is right and good, not what is possible or what will promote the nation's primary interests—its security and prosperity. His opposition to the recognition of Huerta in Mexico showed this motivation; he dictated his position to Mrs. Bryan: "My answer was, first, that I was so unaccustomed to the consideration of public questions separated from both morals and principles of popular government, that I was not able to endorse the view of those who favored the recognition of Huerta."

An editorial in the English *Spectator* on March 21, 1914 was highly critical of Bryan's "optimism and idealism," shown especially in his treaties for the peaceful settlement of disputes. It doubted whether "pious formulae" could find solutions to "international jealousies, meanness, and misunderstanding." Bryan's treaties, the author believed, "will lead to deep disappointment." The editorial continued:

> An excellent example of the kind of optimism we mean is provided in an interview with Mr. Bryan which was published in the *Daily Chronicle* of Tuesday. "Mr. Bryan's eyes" says the interviewer, "shone with the enthusiasm of humanity, his voice throbbed

with the passion for universal peace, as he reeled off to me the successes already achieved in the signing of Arbitration Treaties by thirteen nations."

It was easy for Secretary Bryan to be neutral in World War I and understandable that he would be impatient with evidences of partiality toward Britain and France displayed by Wilson and other colleagues. This firm attitude brought upon him charges of being pro-German. He saw no security interest of the United States involved in the War and appeared unworried that the power balance in Europe had been challenged. His successor, Robert Lansing, was a man of sterner realism, as seen in his attitudes toward the War and toward peace-making, attitudes that got him into trouble with Wilson, whose main concern at the Paris Peace Conference was a League of Nations.

Since 1947, our presidents and secretaries have met world problems with a realism that would do credit to John Quincy Adams, but not without displaying attitudes which the idealist would approve. When facing great danger, they have safeguarded the nation's security by those methods traditionally regarded as realistic—military power and alliances in particular; where it could serve their purposes, they have worked through the United Nations. They have, like most responsible statesmen, used the language of idealism in their public utterances; possibly, in less critical times, their approach to policy would have been that of a Root or a Wilson. American policies under their leadership have not deviated seriously from accepted ethical principles or from legal obligations, communist charges to the contrary notwithstanding. The U-2 trip may be referred to as realistic, but, in view of the closed society of the Soviet Union and the consequent danger of a surprise attack on us (in addition to the general acceptance of intelligence activities everywhere), accusations that it was unethical are not convincing. From a legal point of view, the violation of territorial sovereignty, which it entailed, was more obvious but hardly more real than in other forms of espionage. American nuclear testing in 1962, widely condemned as unethical in many quarters, was a realistic answer to the Soviet violation of a test ban; until then this country had kept its pledge against testing and had even refrained from preparations for tests. Critics of American conduct in the cold war often remark that this nation has handicapped itself by too rigid an adherence to principles of ethics and law; they were, for instance, impatient with our government's tolerance of Russian penetration of Cuba in 1961-1962. Certainly it would be difficult for a fair-minded observer to contend that our government has flouted ethics and law with no qualm of conscience.

Whatever may have been their abstract philosophies of international politics, both Acheson and Dulles met the pressing problems of their administrations with realism. With their Presidents, they gave more heed to the national security and to power politics than any secretary had since William Seward. Both spoke and acted from a conviction that the welfare of the nation can be served at this juncture in history only by power, ethically used, to prevent Soviet Russia from imposing on all a form of society in which ideals, ethics, and religion would be forever lost.

The word "security" occupied a prominent place in the statements of the two Secretaries whether they were talking to Congressional committees or to the public. Together with idealistic statements, and outnumbering them by far, were frank and forthright assertions of the dangers to the nation, its defense needs, and the power moves taken or to be taken for the protection of the free world. Acheson declared before the Senate Foreign Relations Committee, on March 30, 1950, that "All the things we do are, in the last analysis, measures of national security." He identified the security of Europe with our own, saying to the same Committee on another occasion that ". . . our own security is immeasurably advanced by the strengthening of Western Europe to resist aggression." He saw our protection tied up with that of Germany and the status of Berlin.

The realistic approach of Dean Acheson as Secretary of State was expressed primarily in the effect he gave to "containment" as a policy. By promoting NATO, by aid to our allies, and by acquiring military bases abroad he set up in Europe a ring of power which has played a vital part in deterring further Russian expansion. His realism showed up in the Government's attitude to the Korean problem. After making a statement which some people later interpreted—perhaps unfairly—as implying that American security interests did not include Korea, the Acheson-Truman team committed themselves in 1950, when the Communists attacked, to the defense of that country. Secretary Dulles, in discussing his "brinkmanship" theory, referred to this as an occasion when it would have been better to warn in advance than to come in with a war later on.

Rather pathetically, Secretary Dulles gave voice to the idealism which he claimed to be his guide in his letter of resignation to the President. He regretted that international communism had kept him so busy that he had been unable to build the better world he had always hoped for. His note contained the following statement:

> I was brought up in the belief that this nation of ours was not merely a self-serving society but was founded with a mission to help build a world where liberty and justice would prevail. Today that concept faces a formidable and ruthless challenge from International Communism. This has made it manifestly difficult to adhere steadfastly to our national idealism and national mission and at the same time avoid the awful catastrophe of war.

An idealist by nature, Dulles apparently became a realist by necessity.

Although, as James Reston has expressed it, Secretary Dulles had "a fatal habit of covering up the most obvious power plays with a kind of sanctimonious moralizing," there were many occasions when he talked about his power moves without any sugar-coating whatsoever. One such occasion was in a radio and television address to the nation on May 7, 1954, after returning home from the Geneva Conference. With the aid of a map which television viewers could see, he pointed out the strategic importance to the free world of Indo-China and explained what we had done there. He said frankly, "Throughout this period the United States has also followed the . . . course of trying to develop strength in Southeast Asia through collective measures."

In an interview, the substance of which was published in *Life* magazine on January 16, 1956, Secretary Dulles disclosed a conception of realistic power politics which shocked many Americans. His philosophy has since been referred to by his critics as "brinkmanship." The substance of his statement was that to prevent aggression or to stop it he had three times threatened an evildoer: (1) to bring peace in Korea when armistice negotiations were stalled; (2) to keep Communist China from active intervention in Indo-China; and (3) to save Quemoy and the Matsus from falling into the hands of the Reds. Wars have been started, so Dulles believed, by national leaders who thought they could get away with it—Hitler, for instance—and, when they found out the array of nations which ultimately came to oppose them, it was too late to turn back. He admitted that nobody could prove that his "policy of deterrence" had been the deciding factor in the three instances in which he said he had applied it, but he felt there was "a pretty fair inference" in favor of that conclusion. He said to his interviewer that "You have to take chances for peace, just as you have to take chances in war" and that, in preventing war, "If you are scared to go to the brink, you are lost. . . ."

Secretary Dulles's "massive retaliation" doctrine was another phase of his philosophy of realistic power politics which was widely criticized; Dean Acheson, for instance, did not like it at all, pointing out that it created consternation among our allies. Dulles described his theory to the Council of Foreign Relations on January 12, 1954, and a little later he said more about it to the Foreign Affairs Committee of the House of Representatives. The substance of it was that an enemy, picking his time and place of attack, could force us into action anywhere, and if we were to follow the traditional policy of meeting aggression "by direct and local opposition—then we needed to be ready to fight in the Arctic and in the Tropics; in Asia, the Near East, and in Europe; by sea, by land and by air; with old weapons and with new weapons." This would be very expensive and oblige us to scatter our strength so that it would be thin everywhere. Therefore the National Security Council had decided "to depend primarily upon a great capacity to retaliate instantly, by means and places of our choosing." This, too, was tough power politics, and it led many Americans to fear that a minor incident might be turned into a devastating world war. While to some people it seemed too tough, to others it looked like bluff, for certainly our government would hesitate to start a major war over a minor incident. In the face of this criticism, the Secretary explained in an article for *Foreign Affairs* in April that he was not contemplating an attack on Moscow but only retaliation of a nature calculated to make a communist attack unprofitable.

Dulles, in harmony with the Republican platform of 1952, denounced "containment" as too passive and advocated a stronger policy seeking the "liberation" of peoples in the satellite areas. Again, it seemed that his program was more dynamic than the Acheson-Truman realism. Pressed for details, however, Dulles had nothing specific to offer, and in practice he adhered substantially to the containment policy of his predecessor, extending it to the Asian and Far Eastern fronts.

· XII ·

His Living Office

The dynamic quality exhibited by the office of secretary of state throughout its history, its capacity to adjust and develop, has been frequently noted in this book. The office, like the nation it serves, has gone through the eras of the stagecoach and the steam locomotive into the present age of the jet-propelled airplane. Now the office is as different from what it was when Thomas Jefferson stepped into it as the United States of 1963 is unlike the infant nation of 1790. And yet in its fundamental aspects the post has remained much the same: it still operates on the basis of the law of 1789; it continues to take whatever role the president may prescribe; as in the past, it gives effect to foreign policy through subordinates in the State Department and foreign service; in short, it remains now as always at the center of the American effort in world affairs. Where the office differs so strikingly from what it was at the beginning is not in its central purpose but (1) in the range of duties and activities undertaken to fulfill that purpose and (2) in the relationships which it has been obliged to work out with the National Security

Council and other agencies with whom it and the Department of State have come to share policy-advising duties.

Devoted to much the same objective but with different techniques, the office has been revolutionized in its routine. The more complicated world in which the secretary carries on plus the deeper involvement of this nation in the world's vicissitudes have combined to place on his desk problems so numerous and profound as to force him into a complete reorganization of his work. He can give no time to the kind of details that occupied John Quincy Adams—organizing a filing system for letters, handling claims of Americans against foreign governments, planning a reorganization of the Department's library, and on occasion even writing out the drafts of treaties himself. Increasingly, he has had to rely on the facilities of the Department, even in his advice to the president on policy where it supplies him with the data and ideas he needs to do his thinking. The gigantic policy-making machine of which he is a part, and the most important individual member aside from the president, requires him to be in close touch not only with high officials in his Department, but also with the National Security Council and a vast array of interdepartmental committees and boards. Since 1949 the policy-making structure in which he carries on has embraced our allies and imposed upon him the duty of consulting with them either separately or in the organs of NATO, SEATO, or the Organization of American States.

Earlier chapters have pointed out other ways in which Mr. Secretary of State has had to adjust himself to the demands of the times. To court the Congressional backing that has become imperative if his policies are to be made effective and his Department kept at top efficiency, he and his subordinates have devoted themselves with increasing zeal. Anxious to transform his policies from a partisan to a national basis and in this way to give them the strength needed in the treacherous world of today, he finds himself less implicated in party politics and inclined even in his political contacts with Congress to cross party lines. The new diplomacy, founded upon an expanded interest of the people in foreign affairs and their determination to play an active part in decision-making, has compelled him to make more public addresses, to hold press conferences, and to set up in his Department the agencies needed to help him shape public opinion as well as to listen to it. The modern style of diplomacy has forced him to work more in the open and thus has limited his flexibility in dealing with other nations and his ability to make the kind of compromises which are essential to successful negotiations. It has at the same time enhanced his role as a negotiator by its emphasis upon top-level—summit and subsummit—negotiating. To carry on as the nation's most active negotiator and to make the personal contacts on good-will trips which modern diplomacy emphasizes, he has become a world traveler, perhaps even more than the circumstances have demanded. Busy with world-shaking problems he has little time to keep his Department in working order; he is less of an administrator than formerly, and, although he makes major decisions on the organization of the Department, most of this phase of his responsibilities must now be handled by under secretaries or assistant secretaries.

Like the office itself, the president's concept of it has changed. He, too, has grown busier; with less time for details, he, too, must rely more upon subordinates. In foreign affairs this tends to enlarge the role of the secretary of state as well as to call for the help of the National Security Council and other agencies. As an adviser on foreign policy, the secretary is less expendable than formerly for the further reason that international problems are more numerous and more complex than in the days when this nation was relatively detached from world affairs. The president may still be his own secretary of state in the sense that he makes the decisions, even against the advice of his secretary; he may still rely on a Harry Hopkins or his White House staff for ideas as much or more than on his secretary. But more than ever the president will insist that the advice coming to him be from a source which is reliable, informed, and responsible. In these respects no single official can compete with the secretary, whose contacts with the State Department, the National Security Council, and other organizations and persons provide him a unique capability. When, late in 1961, certain members of the White House staff, who had been advising the president informally and at times were in disagreement with the secretary of state, were moved to high positions in the State Department and made subordinates of the secretary, it was apparent that anything haphazard or ill-contrived in the system by which the chief executive is advised is now less tolerable than it used to be, even in the time of President Franklin Roosevelt.

More dependent on his secretary's office than ever, the president wants it kept at the highest peak of efficiency. It no longer appears to him in the light of a political plum to be handed to a deserving politician. To an unprecedented degree, especially since World War II, the chief executive has filled the office with men who have been active in diplomacy. The politician-amateur type has recently become rare, perhaps on the way to extinction. This trend fits in neatly with the new pressures upon the secretary to keep his partisan activities while in office at a minimum.

As a person, the secretary himself has been developing along new lines. Now he often possesses a background in diplomacy and is able to look at his problems from the vantage point of experience; he knows how to prepare for and to carry on negotiations; he is acquainted with the high officials of other nations and very likely with members of the American foreign service; and he is in the habit of thinking in terms of policy. Since he is less frequently a lawyer, his outlook on policy problems will be less legalistic and more concerned with the national interest and with the economic, psychological, and other phases of foreign policy. Forced by the inexorable pressures of modern world politics, he has become less idealistic and more realistic in his philosophy.

All told, the realistic diplomat-secretary is better fitted

for every phase of his work except that he may be less well equipped than the politician-amateur for his relations with the people and the Congress. Because his background is not helpful for these contacts and because he is, in any case, too busy with even more important duties to carry much of this burden, his Department should expect to take over more and more of this work. Although the secretary can be greatly relieved by Departmental assistance in these areas of interest, he cannot, however, shake off the duty to make public addresses, to appear before Congressional committees on important policy projects, and to confer with influential Congressmen.

The stature of the office, always high, has in no way diminished as it has grown older. Appointments to it are watched by the public with more interest and concern than to any other post in the government. Its incumbent, even more now than in earlier years, is in the headlines for what he is doing or failing to do. Yet, paradoxically, the prominence of the office no longer assures its incumbent of consideration for the presidency as in the early decades of the Republic. To the contrary, the man in the office of secretary of state has probably gone as high as he will go. He can afford to eschew politics.

Because (1) the office of secretary of state has grown into almost unmanageable proportions, (2) our foreign relations have become more precarious by far, and (3) foreign policy now involves a wider base in technological data—economic, psychological, military, scientific, etc.—than ever before, several proposals have been advanced during the past three or four years looking toward a far-reaching reorganization of the government for its work abroad. These projects have been designed in part to relieve the secretary of some of his duties and thus to give him more time for deliberation on policy. They presume to deal, too, with the problem of producing a unity of action out of the different government departments and agencies whose work has a relationship to that of the State Department: the National Security Council, the Defense Department, the Department of Commerce, the Department of Agriculture, the United States Information Agency, the International Cooperation Administration, and others. They have emanated from such commendable sources as ex-President Hoover, Senator Mansfield, Governor Rockefeller (using the study of the President's Advisory Committee on Government Organization), and the Brookings Institution.

Although these projects differ in detail, all advocate a top man in foreign affairs with more authority than the present secretary of state. Three of them (the Hoover, Mansfield, and Rockefeller suggestions) would have a supercabinet official in foreign affairs—a vice-president for foreign affairs, a first secretary of the government, or a secretary of state with authority over other departments in activities relating to international relations. This high official would be expected, among other things, to represent the United States at international meetings. The Brookings plan does not call for a supercabinet official but would have a secretary of foreign affairs who would be the vice-chairman of the National Security Council and in charge of three other officials with cabinet status: a secretary of state (over the State Department); a secretary for the United States Information Agency; and a secretary for the International Cooperation Administration.

None of these proposals has had wide support; all have seemed too complicating in one respect or another. For one cabinet officer to be able to meddle in the affairs of other cabinet officers, somewhat in the manner of a prime minister, would hardly be acceptable in this country. The plan of the Brookings Institution for three subordinate secretaries, according to Mr. Dean Acheson, would incorporate "the defects of the Defense Department organization into the State Department." Secretary Herter felt that reorganization along any of the above lines was unnecessary and unwise. In his opinion the relationship between the State Department and the other departments is now essentially correct. He opposed a supersecretary of state on the ground that coordinating the work of the three proposed subdivisions would itself be so heavy a task that "Instead of being relieved of burdens, he [the top secretary] might find his load increased." It is significant that two ex-secretaries of state with their experience in foreign affairs should oppose these plans. Significant, too, is the recommendation of the American Assembly that "It would be inadvisable to interpose any official between the President and the Secretary of State in the field of international affairs."

The point is that the adviser to the president can and does profit from the kind of contacts that the secretary now has: his close touch with the State Department's experts and its fund of information; his conversations with the heads of the Defense Department, the Commerce Department, and the others; his presence in interdepartmental boards, in the Cabinet, and in the National Security Council; his discussions with the foreign secretaries and diplomats of other nations; and his talks with Congressmen and other politicians. To divide these rich experiences with a higher official or with others on his own level would be to diminish the capacity of any one of them to advise the president, to negotiate, or to carry on other vital activities in foreign affairs.

The adjustments which can be made to relieve the secretary from his heavy burden of work must be of the kind that free him from details and wasted effort without weakening his hold on any of the controls that keep the foreign-policy machine running. He can help himself by restricting his travels abroad to a necessary minimum, by limiting his speaking engagements to those most useful in maintaining public contacts, and by taking part only in those social affairs that have a relation to his official duties. Attention has been directed to the possibility of diminishing his Congressional contacts. To this end congressmen could contribute by not insisting so often on interviews with the secretary or on his personal testimony before committees (as the American Assembly has suggested), by a more willing cooperation with the administration in its policy programs, and by supplying funds essential to the maintenance of a strong Department of

State. The work of the secretary will always be lightened by a Department operating at top efficiency, and to bring this about he as well as the Congress is in a position of responsibility; his share in this enterprise must in large part, as now, be undertaken by other high officials in his Department. Undoubtedly an understanding public, mindful of its proper role in a healthy democracy, can also be helpful by not demanding the performance of miracles by the secretary, by desisting from showering him with ill-conceived advice which confuses and obstructs without enlightening, by not requiring information on every move that he makes, and by tempering its criticism with restraint.

Although the efficient organization of the processes of policy-making in foreign affairs deserves the careful attention of all concerned, it will always be of secondary importance. Policy-making is inherently a human rather than a mechanical process. If policies are wise, they have been conceived in the minds of wise men; the mechanics of the process are significant only as the means by which that wisdom can be converted into policies. The quality of American foreign policy will always reflect first and foremost the aptitude of the American people and their leaders. A mature people, a wise president, and a capable secretary of state together produce a combination which will assure an effective use of whatever organization and processes are at hand. They can save the nation from its external foes.

Appendix

*The Presidents and Their Secretaries of State**

PRESIDENT	SECRETARY OF STATE
George Washington (*April* 30, 1789—*March* 4, 1797)	John Jay Thomas Jefferson Edmund Randolph Timothy Pickering
John Adams (*March* 4, 1797—*March* 4, 1801)	Timothy Pickering John Marshall
Thomas Jefferson (*March* 4, 1801—*March* 4, 1809)	James Madison
James Madison (*March* 4, 1809—*March* 4, 1817)	Robert Smith James Monroe
James Monroe (*March* 4, 1817—*March* 4, 1825)	John Quincy Adams
John Quincy Adams (*March* 4, 1825—*March* 4, 1829)	Henry Clay
Andrew Jackson (*March* 4, 1829—*March* 4, 1837)	Martin Van Buren Edward Livingston Louis McLane John Forsyth

* The list includes John Jay, who actually served as Secretary of State for about a year under the Constitution although he was not commissioned by President Washington. It lists Daniel Webster twice to cover his two separate terms, and James G. Blaine twice for the same purpose. The list omits secretaries of state ad interim. Note has not been made of occasions when a secretary's term was continued a few days into an incoming administration before a new appointment could be made.

PRESIDENT	SECRETARY OF STATE
Martin Van Buren (*March 4, 1837—March 4, 1841*)	John Forsyth
William Henry Harrison (*March 4, 1841—April 4, 1841*)	Daniel Webster
John Tyler (*April 6, 1841—March 4, 1845*)	Daniel Webster Abel Upshur John Calhoun
James K. Polk (*March 4, 1845—March 4, 1849*)	James Buchanan
Zachary Taylor (*March 4, 1849—July 9, 1850*)	John Clayton
Millard Fillmore (*July 10, 1850—March 4, 1853*)	John Clayton Daniel Webster Edward Everett
Franklin Pierce (*March 4, 1853—March 4, 1857*)	William Marcy
James Buchanan (*March 4, 1857—March 4, 1861*)	Lewis Cass Jeremiah Black
Abraham Lincoln (*March 4, 1861—April 15, 1865*)	William H. Seward
Andrew Johnson (*April 15, 1865—March 4, 1869*)	William H. Seward
Ulysses S. Grant (*March 4, 1869—March 4, 1877*)	Elihu Washburne Hamilton Fish
Rutherford B. Hayes (*March 4, 1877—March 4, 1881*)	William Evarts
James A. Garfield (*March 4, 1881—September 19, 1881*)	James G. Blaine
Chester A. Arthur (*September 19, 1881—March 4, 1885*)	James G. Blaine Frederick Frelinghuysen
Grover Cleveland (*March 4, 1885—March 4, 1889*)	Thomas Bayard

PRESIDENT	SECRETARY OF STATE
Benjamin Harrison (*March 4, 1889—March 4, 1893*)	James G. Blaine John Foster
Grover Cleveland (*March 4, 1893—March 4, 1897*)	Walter Gresham Richard Olney
William McKinley (*March 4, 1897—September 14, 1901*)	John Sherman William Day John Hay
Theodore Roosevelt (*September 14, 1901—March 4, 1909*)	John Hay Elihu Root Robert Bacon
William H. Taft (*March 4, 1909—March 4, 1913*)	Philander Knox
Woodrow Wilson (*March 4, 1913—March 4, 1921*)	William Jennings Bryan Robert Lansing Bainbridge Colby
Warren G. Harding (*March 4, 1921—August 2, 1923*)	Charles Evans Hughes
Calvin Coolidge (*August 3, 1923—March 4, 1929*)	Charles Evans Hughes Frank Kellogg
Herbert C. Hoover (*March 4, 1929—March 4, 1933*)	Henry Stimson
Franklin D. Roosevelt (*March 4, 1933—April 12, 1945*)	Cordell Hull Edward Stettinius, Jr.
Harry S Truman (*April 12, 1945—January 20, 1953*)	Edward Stettinius, Jr. James Byrnes George Marshall Dean Acheson
Dwight D. Eisenhower (*January 20, 1953—January 20, 1961*)	John Foster Dulles Christian Herter
John F. Kennedy (*January 20, 1961*)	Dean Rusk

Bibliography

A useful series of studies on the lives and policies of individual secretaries of state up to 1929 is provided in a ten-volume work edited by Professor Samuel F. Bemis and entitled *The American Secretaries of State and Their Diplomacy* (New York: A. A. Knopf, 1927-1929). A more recent publication, *An Uncertain Tradition* (New York: McGraw-Hill, 1961), edited by Professor Norman A. Graebner, deals with secretaries of state in the twentieth century, giving a brief outline of the career and the major policies of each. In *The Department of State* (New York: Macmillan, 1949), Professor Graham Stuart discusses briefly the career background of each secretary and his work, emphasizing administrative problems and innovations. The American Assembly in 1960 put out a small volume, *The Secretary of State* (Englewood Cliffs, N.J.: Prentice-Hall, 1960), edited by Mr. Don K. Price; it concentrates on the problems of the office. Bibliographical sketches of secretaries up to 1956 may be found in *The Secretaries of State: Portraits and Bibliographical Sketches*, compiled by Richard S. Patterson and published by the Department of State in 1956 as Publication 6402.

Much useful information on the office of secretary of state may be found in general works on the conduct of American foreign relations. The following books of this nature are recommended:

Barron, Bryton, *Inside the State Department: A Candid Appraisal of the Bureaucracy*. New York: Bookmailer, 1956.

Bendiner, Robert, *The Riddle of the State Department*. New York: Farrar and Rinehart, 1942.

Bundy, Harvey, and Rogers, James, *The Organization of the Government for the Conduct of Foreign Affairs*. Washington: Government Printing Office, 1949.

Committee on the Organization of the Executive Branch of the Government (Hoover Committee), *Task Force Report on Foreign Affairs*. Washington: Government Printing Office, 1949.

Hulen, Bertram D., *Inside the Department of State*. New York: McGraw-Hill, 1939.

Levitt, Albert, *The President and the International Affairs of the United States*. Los Angeles: Parker and Co., 1954.

McCamy, James L., *The Administration of American Foreign Affairs*. New York: A. A. Knopf, 1950.

Mathews, John M., *American Foreign Relations: Conduct and Policies*, Revised edition. New York: D. Appleton-Century, 1938.

Plischke, Elmer, *Conduct of American Diplomacy*, Revised edition. Princeton, N.J.: Van Nostrand, 1961.

Snyder, Richard, and Furniss, Edgar, *American Foreign Policy: Formulation, Principles, and Programs*. New York: Holt, Rinehart & Winston, 1954.

Steiner, Zara S., *The State Department and the Foreign Service: The Wriston Report—Four Years Later*. Princeton: Center of International Studies, 1958.

United States Committee on Government Operations, *Organization for National Security: Selected Materials*, 86 Cong. 2nd Session. Washington: Government Printing Office, 1960.

A wealth of material is available on individual secretaries of state in the form of biographies, autobiographies, memoirs, and books on current problems which they have written. The list below is a selected one which relates to a few of the more prominent secretaries of the nineteenth century and those of the twentieth century.

Acheson, Dean G., *A Citizen Looks at Congress*. New York: Harper, 1957.

Acheson, Dean G., *Power and Diplomacy*. Cambridge, Mass.: Harvard University Press, 1958. (Paperback edition, New York: Atheneum, 1962.)

Bancroft, Frederic, *The Life of William H. Seward*. New York: Harper, 1900.

Beal, John R., *John Foster Dulles: 1888-1959*. New York: Harper, 1959.

Bemis, Samuel F., *John Quincy Adams and the Foundations of American Foreign Policy*. New York: A. A. Knopf, 1949.

Bryan, William Jennings, and Bryan, Mary Baird, *Memoirs of William Jennings Bryan*. Philadelphia: John C. Winston, 1925.

Bryn-Jones, David, *Frank B. Kellogg*. New York: G. P. Putnam's Sons, 1937.

Byrnes, James F., *Speaking Frankly*. New York: Harper, 1947.

Dennett, Tyler, *John Hay: From Poetry to Politics*. New York: Dodd, Mead, 1933.

Fuess, Claude M., *Daniel Webster*. Boston: Little, Brown, 1930.

Heller, Deane, *John Foster Dulles, Soldier for Peace*. New York: Holt, Rinehart & Winston, 1960.

Hinton, Harold B., *Cordell Hull, A Biography*. Garden City: Doubleday, 1942.

Hull, Cordell, *The Memoirs of Cordell Hull*, 2 vols. New York: Macmillan, 1948.

Jessup, Philip C., *Elihu Root*. New York: Dodd, Mead, 1938.

Lansing, Robert, *War Memoirs of Robert Lansing, Secretary of State*. New York: Bobbs-Merrill, 1953.

Nevins, Allan (editor), *The Diary of John Quincy Adams, 1794-1845*. New York: Longmans, Green, 1929.

Perkins, Dexter, *Charles Evans Hughes and American*

Democratic Statesmanship. Boston: Little, Brown, 1956.

Pusey, Merlo J., *Charles Evans Hughes*. New York: Macmillan, 1951.

Seward, Frederick W. (editor), *Autobiography of William Henry Seward*. New York: D. Appleton, 1891.

Stimson, Henry L., and Bundy, McGeorge, *On Active Service in War and Peace*. New York: Harper, 1948.

Thayer, William R., *The Life and Letters of John Hay*. Boston: Houghton Mifflin, 1915.

Index